PLANT *your* FLAG

THE SEVEN SECRETS TO WINNING

PLANT *Your* FLAG
THE SEVEN SECRETS TO WINNING

© 2020 Carolyn J Rivera

Published in New York, New York, by Morgan James Publishing. Morgan James is a trademark of Morgan James, LLC. www.MorganJamesPublishing.com

ISBN 9781642795653 paperback
ISBN 9781642795660 eBook
Library of Congress Control Number: 2018910867

Cover Design by:
Tyler Trout
Trout Design

Interior Design by:
SeedStudios.com

Morgan James is a proud partner of Habitat for Humanity Peninsula and Greater Williamsburg. Partners in building since 2006.

Get involved today! Visit
MorganJamesPublishing.com/giving-back

PLANT *Your* FLAG

THE SEVEN SECRETS TO WINNING

CAROLYN J RIVERA

Dedication

I would like to dedicate this book to my loving family. My husband Jo'el, my kids Gabi, Dani and JJ. For everything you do in life, do it with purpose. Step out of your comfort zone and follow your dreams. Live a life of learning and adventure. Believe, Commit, Achieve!

"A good 'Survivor' leader is someone who has the ability to unite a group in a common goal while still pursuing their own individual interests and remaining flexible.

A leader will have the ability to adapt to a changing environment as well as accurately assess the perceptions of themselves and others. This self-awareness skill is often the most important of all!"

–Rob Mariano
'Survivor' Winner, Season 22
Marquesas, All-Stars, "Heroes vs. Villains, Redemption Island"

Acknowledgements

When you set out to write a book you never realize what it takes to make it happen. There are so many people that have inspired me along the way. First, I want to acknowledge my family. I must start by thanking my husband Jo'el. He read every draft, giving me feedback along the way, even when I wasn't ready or didn't want the feedback. Every change you offered, made the book that much better! To my children Gabi, Dani and JJ, you have always supported me in my crazy endeavors and this book is no different. Now that you guys are all grown up, I look forward to bouncing ideas off of you all. I am grateful for the insight each of you provided. Seeing things through your eyes helped me tell the story and you all inspire me every day. My mom Sandee who no matter what crazy thing I come up with has always wanted me to succeed and I know you would do anything for me! My brother Mitch and his wife Kim for providing me with the real-truth on things when I needed it; from titles, to book covers, to pictures that just got a flat-out NO! My, soon to be son-in-law Tyler Trout, who I owe the fabulous design of my front and back cover. His creativity and exceptional talent for graphic design is unmatched. My small but powerful family is my rock!

To my dear friends. Debby Harrington, Judy Mavrakes, Maureen Peschel, Bob Moretti, Kip Knight, Aileen Wilkins. You guys have read my manuscript, some of you several times, provided advice and ideas for making the book better. Thank you for giving me the stories I used in the book, and you know who you are.

Special Thanks goes to Holly Hoffman and Missy Payne for sharing with me all the steps necessary to write a book. For being available when I needed to have questions answered and for providing advice on how to get this book done. You both provided me with fabulous people for my editing and publishing and I am so grateful that I didn't have to search and find those people on my own.

To my editors Corrina Capotrio and Cheryll Duffie. You guys have put so much into making this book a reality. I couldn't have done it without you both. I would have to proclaim you both as the Worlds Best Editors!

To my publisher Russell Lake. Not only for putting it all together but for coming up with the title! It is a perfect fit for the book and I can't thank you enough!

To my "Survivor" family. Mike Holloway, Sandra Diaz-Twine, Rob Mariano, Bob Crowley, Adam Klein, Tina Wesson, Wendell Holland, Jeremy Collins, Michele Fitzgerald, Sarah Lacina. When I called you and asked you to provide me with a quote and the fact that I needed it right away you all came through. Thank you for your friendship, encouragement and support along the way.

Special Thank You!

Jo'el Rivera
Gabrielle Rivera
Danielle Rivera
Jo'el Anthony Rivera
Tyler Trout
Sandee White
Mitch Amkraut
Kim Amkraut
Debby Harrington
Judy Mavrakes
Maureen Peschel
Bob Moretti
Kip Knight
Aileen Wilkins
Holly Hoffman

Missy Payne
Corrina Capotrio
Cheryll Duffie
Russell Lake
Mike Holloway
Rob Mariano
Sandra Diaz-Twine
Bob Crowley
Adam Klein
Tina Wesson
Wendell Holland
Jeremy Collins
Michele Fitzgerald
Sarah Lacina

contents

"Leaders play all different roles.

*They must be capable of adapting
to all situations.*

*They need to be strong and to know how
to make quick decisions.*

*My strategy was always to be one step
ahead of my opponents*

*and to be able to communicate with
people to constantly build alliances.*

Queen stays Queen!"

–Sandra Diaz-Twine
'Survivor' Winner, Seasons 7 and 20
Pearl Islands, Panama, "Heroes vs. Villains,"
and "Game Changers"

Introduction

I believe we all have the ability to be leaders.

I also believe we should all make a commitment to lead where we are—whether on a grand stage before thousands of people or simply within our own personal sphere of influence. We all have the potential to lead whatever our circumstances.

Every one of us has skills, perspective, experiences, and ideas that can be used to help others.

Every one.

Wherever our passions lie, we all have something to contribute to others.

Leadership is clearly not a new concept. The realization of, the intentionality of, and marketing of leadership, however, *is* a relatively new idea. So much so, that you can stick the word 'leadership' in a book title or a conference promo, and you're all but guaranteed to attract attention. Leadership is *the* buzz word of today.

In years past, leadership was thought to be reserved for a select group—the driven, the gifted, the exceptional. And while that is frequently true for those who have gone on to lead companies and countries and organizations, it is also true for the stay-at-home mom of three who is the go-to mom always arranging play dates.

Or the guy in the next cubicle who comes in early and stays late and always seems to be prepared for team meetings.

Or the neighbor who sets up a community website to help raise funds for a nearby park.

Whether they have an official title or a detailed job description *or not,* leaders are everywhere.

In an article for *Training* magazine titled, "Four Types of Leaders,"[1] Professor Paul B. Thornton presented what he believes to be one of the primary characteristics of leaders: "Effective leaders believe that individuals, organizations, and even nations, possess undiscovered talents and untapped resources. They seek to unleash the full potential of their followers so they can reach higher and go farther than they previously thought possible."

Thornton goes on to identify what he considers to be the four types of leaders:

Thought Leaders – "Thought leaders harness the power of ideas to actualize change. They stretch their followers by helping them envision new possibilities…Thought leaders attract followers and initiate change by the power of their ideas." Steve Jobs is an excellent example based upon his tremendous contribution to the digital and technology world. Another example might be head of your child's Parent/Teacher Organization who goes against the annual tradition of a school carnival and instead, plans a community-wide 5K fun run, thereby involving a broader base of participants, raising more money, and increasing awareness of the school's need for additional gym equipment.

Courageous Leaders – "Courageous leaders bravely pursue a vision in the face of considerable opposition and risks. They have strong convictions about their mission (purpose), vision (long-term goals), and values (right and wrong). They speak up for their core beliefs and fight for their values, even when their stand is unpopular." One of the most well-known courageous leaders is Rosa Parks, the African American woman who, in 1955, refused to give up her bus seat for a white person. Even in the face of an uncertain outcome and consequences, Mrs. Parks did what was right and equitable. In the workplace, this might be the woman who reports the sexual harassment of another employee several management levels above her.

Inspirational Leaders – "Inspirational leaders promote change by the power of their passionate commitment to ideas and ideals. They lift our eyes from present practicalities to future possibilities. Their words stir up our spirits, strengthen our convictions, and move us to action. We are eager to follow them because they call forth the best that is in us." The Rev. Martin Luther King is an excellent example of an inspirational leader who brought about historic change through his words and his commitment to nonviolent protests. Closer to home, a local pastor, preacher, or Bible study leader often provides the motivation and inspiration for deepening our spiritual walk.

Servant Leaders – "Servant leaders care deeply about people. They seek to remove the barriers and obstacles that hold others back from achieving their full potential. They strive to create an environment where their followers can do their best work. Servant leaders frequently ask, 'How can I help?'" Mother Teresa is widely recognized as a servant leader who laid the groundwork for thousands of others to follow in her footsteps to serve the poor. Teachers and coaches are usually stellar examples of servant leaders as they tirelessly work to help students become and do their best.

Leadership happens all day, every day, all around us— whether we're cognizant of it or not. Anytime someone takes an idea, shares a plan to put it into place, and makes it happen, they're leading others. Sometimes it's intentional and well-thought out; sometimes it's not. It is present in the workplace, amongst our family members, throughout our communities, neighborhoods, and schools, and within our places of worship. Anywhere people are present, leadership is always in practice.

But here's the catch—leadership is also a dynamic practice. Because it is affected by cultural norms, accepted practices, and widely ranging personalities, *leadership is constantly changing.*

And just as leadership styles shift and shape our society, so also does our personal style of leadership continue to evolve throughout our lives. To excel in leadership, just as it is in any other skill, we must both initially adapt to and ultimately, challenge the status quo.

Just when you think you have become an accomplished master in one area, the bar is raised. The norms are adjusted. Exceptions soon become commonplace. The world around you will always continue to change and so must your leadership.

Some 30 years ago, I remember watching in fascination as Nadia Comaneci dominated the world of gymnastics. She was the undisputed *master* of the sport, going so far as to score a perfect 10 in the 1976 Olympics. At the time, her performance was considered flawless. Today, accomplished gymnasts wouldn't even be considered for the Olympic team with a similar routine because it is so outdated and well below the expected difficulty level of current top tier athletes.

Just as the definition and degree of mastery changes over time in the world of competitive gymnastics, it also changes with leadership styles and practices. The envelope is constantly being pushed to accommodate and improve upon generally accepted levels of excellence, be it on the uneven parallel bars or leading in the conference room. No longer is leadership simply considered leading a group of people towards a common goal. It also implies intentional action and forward thinking with potentially significant benefits. The stakes of leadership can oftentimes be extremely high.

I have devoted my life to learning about leadership and becoming the best possible leader I can be. I work with leaders in all aspects of my day-to-day obligations, intentionally studying how and why they do what they do in order to be most effective. After years of research and practice, I felt called to share what I've learned along the way and a few personal experiences as well. My hope is to inspire the next generation of men and women called to become true leaders.

I have been fortunate to have some great role models in my life who have helped me succeed at all levels of my career. I have also had my fair share of setbacks as well which, looking back, I now realize were necessary for me to continue to learn and grow. I'll share my personal victories as well as the difficulties of my journey. There's a high likelihood you will have heard or been exposed to much of what I present going forward—it's truly not rocket science. However, that said, my goal is to bring these successful leadership concepts to the forefront of your mind and to present them based upon my perspective and experiences.

It's no great secret—we all generally know what it takes to be a successful. We all know that leaders come in all different shapes and sizes. And we all know there is *no one way to lead.* Leadership is situational. However, I have never met a leader who didn't have, at the very least, these three vital traits in common: conviction, passion, and the courage to stand out.

My own personal motto for becoming a leader closely resembles this list. For me, and moving forward throughout this book, I focus on what I consider to be the non-negotiables for leaders. These include an individual's ability to Believe, Commit, and Achieve.

My method of storytelling is through real-life examples everyone can relate to. I want to empower you to begin to consider yourself a focused, effective leader wherever you are.

Ask yourself these questions:

When you think about leadership, what are the characteristics that come to your mind? What do you picture in your mind when you hear the word leadership?

The reason I ask these pointed questions is simple: because our values, beliefs, and experiences all contribute to the paths we choose in life and the people we choose to emulate.

Growing up, I was taught to respect people in positions of authority. This practice was reinforced throughout my many years and experiences in the corporate world. In my early days, I naturally just considered the leader to be the person in charge, at least *officially*. This meant the person in the position of power, usually with the corresponding title. They would be the ones held accountable for a team or department's performance, be it sales, revenue, or resolution of issues. Outside the office, I took this to mean others with position and title such as a coach, a pastor, or an elected official.

But as I grew throughout my life, my perspective changed… *radically.*

After having raised three children (two of which received their MBA's; the other a college graduate), traveling the world, living in a Third World country, relocating seven times (yes, seven!) and becoming a Runner-Up on the Number #1 hit reality show of all time, 'Survivor,' it quickly became apparent—*all* of these experiences have helped to shape who I am today.

From there, I soon realized that leadership—*true leadership*—runs much deeper than just being assigned accountability and authority over others. There is a distinct difference between simply being a *titled* team member and actually *leading* a team. For example, the person in charge of a large ship is responsible for both the well-being of the boat and passengers; he or she usually goes about this by following a prescribed set of instructions and practices. A true leader, on the other hand, will chart the course, set the direction, and instill the confidence necessary within his or crew to ensure a safe arrival.

Leaders are always forward thinkers. They have the ability to create a vision for improving things as they want them to be, *not as they currently are*. Leaders are role models of thought and behavior; their actions oftentimes have a cascading ripple effect on others, inspiring and motivating them to action. And lastly, it is always helpful to understand and accept that leadership is ultimately defined *by others*, and not by you. Even though you can proclaim yourself to be a leader, it is not until you are recognized as such by others that you are truly a leader.

Leaders build strategies to accomplish the future they believe in. They break new ground and change others' lives by envisioning a world of endless possibilities. And they all embody several distinct traits that work together to make them the great leader they have become known as.

In this book, I will focus on the seven specific characteristics I consider essential for you to become the leader you were designed to be and to achieve something we all want— VICTORY!

This book is dedicated to helping *you* achieve VICTORY; to helping *you* gain insight into creating the life *you* want; and to become the kind of leader *you* want to become.

This is not rocket science, friends. This is realistic and attainable *for you, by you.* Every chapter will help better equip you with the tools, behaviors, and specific calls to action that you can work towards incorporating into your everyday life. Sometimes the shifts will seem minimal and the progress almost imperceptible; other times your progress will be substantial, boosting you to greater accomplishments and even higher aspirations. Either way, stick with it. Stay the course. Follow the plan.

And the results? Well, the results will put you squarely on the path to building a VICTORIOUS tomorrow.

"For waging war, you need guidance,
and for victory...many advisors."
–Proverbs 24:6 paraphrased

"VICTORY is the intersection between your unstoppable mindset and your adventurous goals."

–Carolyn J. Rivera

"Leading by example is the first thing that comes to my mind when I think of the definition of Leadership.

People emulate the actions of others.

In the game of Survivor, I wanted to play a fair game which is not easy.

I formed alliances and I kept them which helped me throughout the game.

The Survivor experience gave me a platform to be able to give back.

To form alliances on a much broader scale while helping others in the process.

I have been able to build long lasting relationships with so many people.

To me, that is what leadership is all about.

I am grateful every day for the experience and I would not change it for the world!"

–Bob Crowley
"Survivor" Winner Season 17
Gabon, Central Africa

The reading glasses I used in "Survivor" to create a focused beam of sun light to make a fire. Vision is all about focus!

V is for Vision

Whether you see yourself as a motivated leader of a handful of people or the fearless leader of many, *you must have a vision* of where you want to lead others. Of all the principles I present, this one is truly nonnegotiable. You simply must have a vision—a preferred future, a desired outcome, or a stated goal to lead effectively.

First, allow me to clarify the difference between what I consider to be two distinct types of leaders—motivated and fearless. I define motivated leaders as those with a clearly defined agenda or a cause they are seeking to support. This might be the parent of a special needs child canvassing the neighborhood seeking to educate others about their child's disability. It might also be the district manager wanting to win the coveted Top Region award and the rewards that come with it for her team.

Fearless leaders traditionally are better able to see the potential in others and are able to help them to better believe in themselves all the while striving towards an established goal or set of goals. They know what motivates each member of their team and what methods don't work. They help those they lead by inspiring and encouraging them and help them to believe success is possible based upon what they bring to the team. An accomplished sales manager responsible for his sales reps' quarterly revenue is a prime example of a fearless leader. A successful high school football coach knows where his players excel and places them in the roles where they are most likely to do well—for their sake and the team's.

For some of us, determining our vision comes relatively easy. We have a natural bent that makes pursuing one path over the others seem obvious. We're called to go one direction, work towards a clearly defined goal, or at least explore a general area to focus our energies towards. For others of us, the endless possibilities, options, and paths are overwhelming. There's simply too many paths to consider or roads to travel that we ultimately sit idle—going nowhere because of our inability to choose. We become paralyzed by too many choices.

Wherever you fall on the spectrum of creating a vision for yourself and those whom you lead, defining your vision is critical. Without the direction a vision provides, you will simply spin your wheels; or to quote an old phrase, you'll find yourself, "going nowhere fast." Certainly that's not what you want for your life, your family, and others you lead. In a Harvard Business Review article, "Building Your Company's Vision,[2]" leadership experts Jim Collins and Jerry I. Porras presented what they consider to be the two necessary steps towards crafting a vision:

2

» Define what you stand for and why you exist
» Articulate your aspirations for the future

Two steps. How hard could that be? For plenty of us, these deep, deep questions cause us to become consumed with two very personal aspects of our life—*our past and our future.* We get lost in what has happened in our lives up to this point. We obsess over wrong decisions. We wallow in regret for choices not made, actions not taken. *Or,* we move into overload at the thought of doing everything all at once in an effort to make significant progress. We want what we want and we want to make it happen *now.* We may not know what we're aiming for or where we're trying to get, but we get busy making progress *of some sort.*

So yes, crafting your vision involves only two simple and straightforward challenges . But, they're *doozies!*

Many would-be leaders never get past this very first step. They simply can't commit fully *to a single vision.* They can't see the process of creating a vision because they can't identify and refine *one fully formed idea.* The consideration of all the options leads them to the completion of *none.*

And that's tragic.

And maybe that's been you in the past.

But it doesn't have to be you moving forward.

Because your vision will be different from mine, your neighbor, your coworker, and *everyone else in your life,* this is an intensely personal assignment. It's not something that can be done by *anyone but you.* Otherwise, you would be pursuing *someone else's* vision, and while it may get you to where *they want to be,* it won't take you to where *you want to be.* And isn't that what this one, singular life of ours is all about?

That said, I can provide the next best thing: some personal testimonies as to what has worked for me and a few ordered steps to take towards further identifying what could ultimately be the calling upon your life. Let's get started:

For me, creating and refining my vision for who I am, what I want to do, and what I want to accomplish is a way of life. I am one of the fortunate ones because considering the possibilities and establishing goals comes easy to me. In fact, I actually find it empowering and motivating. Sure, I can get overwhelmed sometimes by thoughts of "I can do this…and this…and that…and that…" And before I know it, I find myself unable to pursue *any* of it because my vision is just too broad. That's when I circle back to what excites me, what motivates me, and what I believe to bring me the greatest joy. The whole visioning process gives me the opportunity to fully open my heart and mind and frees my brain to consider *all* the possibilities available to me.

For me, this usually manifests itself in my passion to challenge the status quo. I am constantly looking for and working towards ways to change and advance and learn and grow. If something is important enough to me, whatever the idea, I don't allow difficulties to stand in my way. I simply consider them opportunities to further strengthen my resolve towards fulfilling my vision. I am able to do this because I have determined what is of tremendous importance to me, and created plans to make them happen. Without either of these two critical steps—the determining and the planning—I wouldn't know which goal to pursue nor how to accomplish *anything.*

And the first step you must take—even before defining who you are and what you stand for or designing a plan to help you travel life's roads is this: Believe.

You must believe in yourself.
You must believe in your dreams.
And you must believe in your ability to accomplish them.
Don't sell yourself short. Don't doubt your abilities, underestimate your resourcefulness, or doubt your commitment.

When you are able to clearly articulate your vision, you are, in effect, taking the first steps towards accomplishing it. When you have a vision, you are empowered. You are strengthened. You become energized and inspired to make it happen. Regardless of whether you're a motivational leader of few or a fearless leader of many, your vision will be the catalyst upon which you and those you lead will rely.

How to Get from Here to There –

As I mentioned earlier, this whole vision-casting process is something I come by easy. Maybe it's my daredevil side or my need to do what others would consider highly improbable (Hello! I was a contestant on 'Survivor!'), if not impossible. Or maybe it's just my personal make-up. Whatever it is, I've had lots of experience when it comes to working through the vision crafting process and helping others do so as well. As such, I've gone so far as to create the numbered list of the steps I follow and those I lead my coaching clients through. These steps have worked *repeatedly*—both for me and countless others. They can also work *for you.*

The necessary steps towards creating and fulfilling your vision –
1. Determine your type of vision
2. Identify the importance of your vision
3. Define and visualize your expected outcomes
4. Communicate the vision with passion and energy
5. Build a movement of inspired champions

Allow me to unpack these further –

Step 1 – Determine Your Type of Vision –

In my experience, I have come to determine what I consider to be the three primary types of vision – personal, career-focused, and business-driven. Each is distinctly different and each brings with it unique dynamics, roles, and responsibilities for those creating them. Of these three, I consider an individual's *personal* vision to be the most important because it provides the foundation upon which the other two kinds of vision can be built.

I believe a personal vision should be a priority for everyone because it is something we *alone* can take responsibility for. Lack of fulfillment can't be blamed on anyone else nor can credit for accomplishment be attributed to anyone else—that's what makes it so *important* and so *personal*. Personal visions keep our minds fresh and our motivations at the forefront of our thoughts and actions. A personal vision is a sort of accountability partner between you and your conscience.

Personal visions can run the gamut from the over-the-top, grand adventure to something much more subtle and intimate. Becoming a top tier athlete would be a bold and tremendously challenging vision to cast for yourself. But just as acceptable (and a lot less exhausting!) would be a commitment to volunteer at your community's food pantry once a week as a means of making a more substantial contribution to your city. Both are challenges. Both require changing your patterns of behavior. Both require intentional commitments of time and energy. Both set the stage for personal fulfillment even if they are just partially accomplished.

And both are valid, rewarding, and viable considerations for a personal vision.

A Personal Turn-out

One of the earliest personal visions I can recall goes all the way back to my teenage years in Queens, New York. When I was in junior high and high school, there were very limited opportunities for girls to participate in organized sports. It just wasn't the norm it is today. Boys were encouraged to play sports, girls were directed towards ballet.

Even though I studied and practiced ballet for seven years, from ages four to eleven, I always knew ballet was not my passion. Still, I waited four more years after quitting ballet to explore and participate in my first organized sport. My high school offered six options for girls to play sports: track, tennis, volleyball, basketball, softball, and handball. The one sport I had become passionate about—gymnastics—was only made available to boys.

All my life, I had watched and grown more and more passionate about gymnastics. It was my dream. I absolutely idolized Nadia Comaneci. And it seemed completely and utterly unfair to my 15-year-old self that girls were not allowed to participate in competitive gymnastics at my school.

So I took what I considered to be the obvious next step: I tried out for the boys' team.

I showed up for tryouts much to the shock and confusion of everyone in the gym that day. Some of the guys tried to direct me to the girls' gym and a few of the coaches wondered if I was pulling some kind of stunt. *Everyone* wondered what I was up to.

Not to be deterred, I let it be known I knew precisely where I was and what my intentions were—to try out for the school's only competitive gymnastics team—*the boys' team.*

I got to work concentrating on floor exercises and the vaulting horse. I knew I didn't quite have the upper body strength to handle the parallel bars or the rings...yet, so I stuck with what I knew. Or rather what I had *watched.* You see, to this point, I had actually never *done* gymnastics. I had watched endless hours of gymnastics on television and I had followed the careers of the elite gymnasts of the day, but beyond that, my gymnastic mastery included a cartwheel.

Nothing else.

A cartwheel.

Still, I knew I was passionate about learning the sport and getting better at it, and what better place to do so than at school? On a team? *With boys?*

And so I did.

I went to tryouts every day that week and a funny thing happened—the more I showed up, the less I stood out. It didn't seem to bother the boys working out. In fact, I think they actually enjoyed it. They even started helping me—spotting me for stunts, helping me on my back handspring, and offering hints for improvement. I was making progress on the mat and with who I hoped would be my future teammates.

But it wasn't to be so easy. By the end of the week I was called into the principal's office as was the gymnastics coach. First, the principal turned to me and asked two very pointed questions: "Why do you want to be on the boys' gymnastics team?" and "Why should I let you join the team?" I knew enough to think things through before I answered, but then I took a deep breath and began: "You should let me be on the boys' team because there isn't a girls' team," I said. "And I really want to compete in gymnastics. And second, you should let me be on the team for two reasons—because it's not fair that, just because I'm a girl, I can't compete on the team, and two, I'm better than lots of the boys trying out!"

He paused before turning to the coach and asking him, "Why should I let Carolyn join the boys' gymnastics team?"

To my surprise, the coach echoed what I had just said, "There is no girls' team and she really is better than some of the boys trying out!"

Right then and there I knew I had an advocate who would stand behind me and champion my cause. I was shocked and grateful. After that, I was given permission to compete on the team representing my high school. It was a huge victory for me in so many ways. I learned the value in following through on a personal vision and I was able to convey my passion and willingness to learn to those in authority. And it ultimately changed the future of girls' sports at my high school.

Oh, and I met my future husband on the team!

One personal vision led to tremendous change for me and for the many girls who came after me. This was the beginning of me understanding the value in three simple words:

Believe.

Commit.

Achieve.

Fulfilling this personal vision and achieving this victory set me on a path that has become a never-ending journey. And I'm grateful for that. It has helped me to see that reaching one personal vision doesn't mean I'm done; it just means it's time to start re-focusing on *a new vision.*

To make the most of this precious one life we're all given, it's important to value the present *and* look ahead to casting *our next personal vision.* Don't ever consider yourself done or beyond learning a new skill or understanding a new perspective. Consider a new challenge. Seek out new passions. Set loftier goals.

I have spent my entire life setting goals and reaching benchmarks, exploring my passion at the moment, and utilizing my gifts and strengths to get to where I wanted to be *next.* And I wouldn't have it any other way. I've gone places I only dreamed about visiting, I've met people I would never have met otherwise, I've grown tremendously in my personal confidence and self-awareness, and, *the bonus,* I've influenced thousands of people along the way to create and follow their own personal vision.

My Most Challenging Personal Goal to Date –

Remember way back to the year 2000? Everybody was all jazzed about a new century, what the 'big 2-0' would do to our computers, and what the new millennium would bring with it.

Not me.

I was front and center watching (and re-watching) *every single episode* of CBS' new reality show, 'Survivor.' They had me from the start. It was a game of true 'survival of the fittest' and I was confident I could compete athletically, strategically, and relationally. In my heart, I knew I was made for this game.

From the start, I wanted to be *on that show.* I studied the early participants and analyzed their strategies. I took note of what worked for them and what didn't. The more I watched and learned, the more compelled I felt to do whatever it took to become a contestant. I don't know what it was (other than the attractive $1,000,000 prize money), that motivated me so relentlessly to put together a plan that would land me on a remote, uncivilized island with 17 people I could trust as far as I could throw them.

What can I say? When I know what I want, *I know what I want.*

It didn't take me long to find out the show struck a chord with lots of people—millions, in fact. I'm not sure if it was the chance for notoriety and exposure on national TV to prove one's physical strength and mental toughness that attracted so many people or the tremendous prize money that was the big draw, but either way, since the very beginning, the competition just to tryout has been fierce and lengthy. It's actually a good thing the whole application process is so intense because it acts as sort of a precursor for the actual competition, weeding out those not fully committed. Because, believe me, if you can't last through the process, you've got no business signing up to be shipped out to *nowheresville*.

As much as I was taken aback by the sheer number of people who applied all over the country, I wasn't discouraged. I knew I had something that all these other wannabe applicants didn't have—and that was my drive and tenacity and unrelenting desire to be selected. Someone else might have an advantage on me in other areas, but *nobody* could match my commitment to seeing this vision through to completion. However, besides the drive and ambition to be selected for the show, I also had something else not all the applicants had—three young children at home. And as kids do, they were all actively engaged in school and sports which meant they needed a mom present and accessible at a moment's notice, not whenever she was released from a television show. Something had to give—my kids or my hope to make it to 'Survivor.' As any mom knows, it wasn't even a choice—my kids would always take priority.

So I put the vision on hold for a few years. But I didn't give up. I used the next few years to gain a better understanding of the show and what it was that set the eventual winners apart from the others. I paid particular attention to the natural outcome of the tribe mentality and the alliances that formed and those that were broken. It was a fascinating study in human behavior and how we respond to extreme adversities—mentally, physically, and most certainly emotionally. I later came to appreciate that it was easy to make assumptions about yourself, your would-be methods, and your perfect strategies from the comfort of your living room couch but it's infinitely harder (on every level) to do so when you haven't slept or eaten sufficiently for three weeks and you don't have the security of trusted relationships.

Hear me on this: be merciful and sparse in your judgment of others; I am living proof you never really know how you would react until you live in someone else's life through and through.

Years passed and my kids had naturally become increasingly more independent. With my two girls in college and my son a junior in high school, I decided the time was right to put some action behind this vision. And let's just say, I'm glad I began when I did, because the whole application process took *years!*

My first attempt was less than stellar. In fact, it was downright disastrous! I flew to New Jersey for an open casting call and that's when I first realized the magnitude of the show's popularity. I had convinced a lifelong friend, Judy, to make the trek with me as she was always up for an adventure. Through the years we had traveled together for work, but our friendship went well beyond our company responsibilities. We had literally traveled the world together and become kindred adventure seekers. Together, we had visited the Taj Mahal, climbed the Great Wall of China, ridden a tiger in Manila, and navigated a river in Asia. What could be so hard about showing up for a television tryout?

To say we were shocked by the turnout and the intensity of the people who had shown up for the open call would be a gross understatement. There was literally a sea of people surrounding the hotel where the auditions were being held. The line of hopefuls wrapped around the hotel, spilling out onto the boardwalk and beyond. It was a five-hour wait just to make it to the door. So we did the obvious next step: we parked our lawn chairs in line and began making friends.

More than five hours after arriving, I was close to 'my moment'—60 whole seconds to answer one single question and to set myself apart from the thousands of others who had waited in line alongside of me. Remember, I had had five-plus hours to think about this, to craft a clever answer, and to take my moment to shine. You'd think my passion alone would have been enough, but not so much. At all.

When I finally made it before the scouts, I choked. Big time. I fumbled for words, appeared ill-prepared, and managed to give them an acceptable answer. The thing is—they weren't looking for *acceptable,* they were looking for *exceptional.*

But despite my mediocre audition, I came away from the experience with a valuable perspective: visions can (and should) be a challenge and a significant reach outside our everyday comings and goings. A vision should take effort. And calculated work. And consistent progress. Otherwise, you're doing little more than climbing a hill when it's the mountain that's the real challenge. Big visions bring big fulfillment.

I also realized I had lost focus on my personal mantra:
Believe.
Commit.
Achieve.

I did believe in myself, but I had not committed to take the steps necessary to make things happen. There's a big difference between believing you can do something and actually moving forward to make it happen. Next time, I would know and do better.

Next time? Most people assumed I would give up on my dream and move on to other pursuits. Most people were wrong. Not only did I recommit to being selected for the show, I thought it through this time. I researched alternative ways of applying. And I created an action plan towards this end.

Because the producers also consider contestants who submit video applications on a very limited basis, I got to work… or rather my family got to work alongside of me. My husband and son both jumped on board with the video idea, one filming and the other one editing. I was responsible for the script—you know, those 60 seconds worth of words that had the power to make me stand out and swing the selection process in my favor. *No pressure!*

As soon as the production company opened the online application process, I submitted my video and, unbelievably, I received a call later *that day.* I was traveling for business and missed the call. I couldn't believe my ears when I checked messages later in the day. I called back immediately. Again and again. And again. But because it was on a Friday, I knew my chances of getting through were next to nil. And I was right.

I probably called back more than a 100 times the following week and left lots of messages—too many. I eventually heard back from my contact person but he was not impressed by my enthusiasm. In the end, I wasn't selected for that season. Or the next several. In fact, it took me four years to finally be chosen but I always remained convinced I would achieve this vision. And then it happened. It was Year 15, Season 30. of the series and I received the call. *The Call.*

Before I knew it, I was partnered with 17 complete strangers (plus a few dozen from the production crew) and shipped off to the jungles of Nicaragua to compete in the 'Worlds Apart' season of 'Survivor.' I was on-site 39 days and earned the nickname 'Mama C' because I was the oldest competitor on the show that season. I finished as a runner-up and took with me experiences and perspective that I have since used to follow further and more ambitious visions. It's no exaggeration to say "Survivor" and my time as a contestant changed the trajectory of my life.

It took incredible planning and accommodations by my family, friends, and coworkers. I regularly practiced visualization to best prepare for what would become the challenge of a lifetime. It tested my commitment level to such a deeply personal undertaking *for years.* And I'd do it all over in a heartbeat because it proved to me, once again, the incredible power that comes from *believing* and *committing* on the way to *achieving* your vision.

Career-focused Vision –

If you hope to move beyond what you are doing today professionally, you must have a career-focused vision. Otherwise, the days will turn into weeks, months, and eventually years, and you'll look back with regret for not being more far-sighted and proactive in the planning of your career path. You'll miss opportunities. You'll be overlooked for significant advancements. And even though you may be considered reliable during your tenure, without a forward-thinking plan for what you want to be doing next year, next decade, or possibly even by the time you retire, you won't be thought of as innovative or insightful or possibly even progressive.

It is far too easy to become comfortable and complacent once you learn the ropes of your particular job or profession. Routine is easy. It's predictable. It affords you the luxury of knowing what to expect from one day to the next or one season to the next.

Comfort and ease of mastery can also be the death knell of advancing and improving and growing as an individual. And trust me, no one at the end of their life ever said, "Gee, I wish I'd never learned anything new or tried my hand at something different."

A career-focused vision is a singular pursuit; no one can do it for you. *You* are the only one who knows what you want deep inside. You're the only one who knows your wildest dreams and hopes for the future. It's a tremendous personal responsibility. It's also a tremendous privilege.

A Personal Turn-out

Years ago, fresh out of college, I set as a career goal to become a vice president at the bank I had been working at part-time. I didn't know exactly *how* I was going to accomplish this, but I did know I wanted it to happen sooner rather than later. Like by the time I was 30.

Once I was promoted to full-time as an assistant manager within the training department, my first action steps were simple: to take the initiative in professional situations whenever appropriate, to learn everything I could about the banking industry (and my institution in particular), and to seek out mentors who could lead and advise me throughout my journey.

I quickly came to appreciate how incredibly valuable this team of advisers could and would become to helping me fulfill my vision. I even gave them a name—my own personal network of champions. These men and women were further along in their career progression, but they had all started where I currently was—*at the bottom* of the management chain. I knew they had learned the system, navigated office politics, and had been rewarded as a result.

And I wanted to know *how they did it.*

One woman, Debby, took a special interest in me. She encouraged me to take on bigger projects as they came my way and assume more responsibility whenever given the opportunity. In doing so, she said, my skillset would grow, I'd gain credibility from those I worked with, and my confidence would soar. She also worked to help me gain a degree of visibility amongst the senior leadership team. As a result of working hard to follow through on her sound advice, I not only survived a company merger and substantial layoffs, but I actually thrived. I accepted transfers and promotions as well as the chance to *really* get out of my comfort zone when I was named a branch manager.

This promotion was a huge step in accomplishing my first career vision because it would take me from back office operations to the front line, interacting with both employees and customers. This was literally an opportunity from the ground up as it was an entirely new branch—not even built yet. I was called upon to give my input into the design of the building, to completely staff it, and to become the face of the branch to our public. I was also *way* out of my comfort zone.

Still, I knew it was the right thing to do if I was truly intent on realizing my vision. It was scary and exciting, risky but fulfilling. It was also one of the most worthwhile professional experiences of my life.

I made the commitment and never looked back. I found I had talent for creating a welcoming environment, both for my employees and our customers. I discovered I loved the sense of accomplishment when I made a successful sale or brought in a new customer. I was challenged *every single day* but I was also frequently rewarded by seeing my name among the company's top-producing branch managers.

I ultimately accepted the position to another, larger branch—again, a risk and a reach well past what I had become accustomed to. But with this promotion, I was also named a company vice president and thrust into many more responsibilities the title brought with it. But I was ready for the challenge. I had sought the advice of others, worked diligently to learn everything I could along the way, and overcome my fair share of professional obstacles through the years. The reward and sense of accomplishment that came from receiving the title and reaching my vision was worth every ounce of effort I put into it. And I wasn't even 30 yet!

Business-driven Vision –

As the name implies, these visions are all about business—making sales, growing market share, constantly innovating. These visions are usually the product of those ultimately held responsible for a company's well-being. It can be mom-and-pop business owners, district/regional/national team leaders, and CEOs. If you are charged with a company's viability, financial health, or brand awareness, chances are you have a business-driven vision.

And if you don't, you need one *immediately.*

Frequently, this type of vision is the most complex as it usually involves many different levels within an organization. Everyone who reports to you (and those that report to them and so on) contributes to the success or failure of a company's ability to achieve its business vision. In order to best accomplish a business vision, everyone has to fully understand it. It must be clear and well-defined, succinct, and have clear lines of authority and accountability in place. The more specifically defined the vision is and the better the communication used to convey it, the greater the odds you and your team will realize the vision. Business visions without these criteria in place rarely succeed.

A Personal Turn-out

Not long ago, I set for myself to establish my own leadership consulting firm. I wanted to create a brand and become a published book author too. After having spent my entire career in the corporate world, I had a lifetime of valuable experience I wanted to share. I had a track record of nearly 30 years leading departments for large organizations. I knew what it took to develop great teams that worked together well. And I had a substantial history of reaching and exceeding more company goals than I could ever count. The work ethic and record of success weren't the challenge; the regular paycheck and luxuries such as insurances and 401k plans were the bigger hurdle for me.

Going out on my own would mean lots of changes, not the least of which would involve hustling *every day* for new business. However, I was somewhat hopeful that after my experience on 'Survivor,' the exposure would go a long way towards opening doors and establishing a recognizable brand and name. I knew the longer the amount of time since my appearance on 'Survivor,' the less weight it would pull in terms of notoriety. I knew the time to get serious about creating a business-driven vision featuring myself as the product—a one-woman-show, so to speak—was *now.*

And so I got to work.

I relied upon my many years working for others and all I had learned about effectively leading others towards continual improvement. I knew strategies and theories and best practices. Now all I had to do was convince others I could present much of what I had learned in order to help *their* people become more fully invested in *their* company's growth.

In the beginning, I didn't charge for speaking engagements. I figured it was an opportunity to hone my presentation skills further and refine my keynote talks. It was a win-win for both the companies I served and myself. Although I had been making professional presentations my entire career, it had always been on behalf of the company I was representing. I was telling *their* stories, pitching *their* products, and promoting *their* ideas. I knew in my heart it was time *to tell my own story.*

It wasn't long before my speaking career took off. Just as I had hoped, my exposure on "Survivor" opened many doors that might not have opened so readily. I soon learned my association with the program brought with it tremendous 'street cred' because it meant I had been considered worthy enough by network executives to appear on their show. I thought it best to ride this wave of recognition as long as possible. I worked to extend my association with "Survivor" by making guest appearances across the country at charitable events.

I made contacts at every stop along the way. I worked hard to maintain relationships with old friends and new. And I began to refine the presentation I would base my message upon. My plan was to help others by motivating them to move past their comfort zones to become better leaders and I planned to show them how through a three-step process and with three simple words:

Believe.
Commit.
Achieve.
My motto became "Ignite Your Will to Win."

I had ignited my own personal will to win in this new venture and was passionate about helping others becoming just as passionate about *their* vision for their life.

Step 2 – Identify the Importance of Your Vision –

Before taking even the first step towards achieving your vision—be it personal, career, or business-related, it is essential to ask yourself a few very important questions:

» Why is this vision important to me personally?
» Is this something that would be nice to accomplish or is it considered a top priority in my life?
» How strong do I feel about the vision I'm creating?
» Am I willing to do whatever it takes to achieve this vision?
» If I don't achieve this vision, how will it affect me personally?

You already know that achieving your vision is going to be hard work—*very hard work.* It will take time (more than you expect), tireless effort, endless dedication, and usually the support of many others along the way. Though it should be obvious by now, it bears stating outright:

» Without an unyielding level of commitment to your vision, you are simply wasting your time.

Your personal level of commitment sets a metaphorical compass that will become your first step towards success. There will undoubtedly be bumps along the road, some foreseeable and planned for, others that seem to come from out of the blue. People will doubt you, your passion, and your means of going about pursuing your vision. They'll question your decision-making and motivation. Even those closest to you may not fully understand what you are doing and voice their concern for how it will affect *them*. But none of this will matter if your vision is truly something you cannot live without pursuing.

Take steps to surround yourself with those who do support you whether they can appreciate your end goal or not. If possible, limit your contact with the naysayers and those who voice their doubts about your vision and your abilities. If these are immediate family members or close work associates, focus on discussing matters with them about *them* and where they place *their* priorities. It can be enlightening and it takes the scrutiny away from your pursuits.

Throughout my life there have been many times when people haven't understood or didn't agree with my vision. Applying for "Survivor" once would be near the top of that list. Applying four times would be at *the top* of the list.

For me, being selected as a contestant for the show was among my top visions. I truly felt I should give the whole applications process (time after time!) everything I could. And then, if never chosen, I could rest in the knowledge that I had done everything I possibly could to reach my vision. My vision for appearing on "Survivor" was crystal clear—do everything within my power to make it happen.

This is precisely the kind of commitment *you* must have in whatever vision you hold for yourself.

Step 3 – Define and Visualize the Expected Outcome–

With the creative, self-reflecting process behind you, you are now free to identify some goals to mark and measure your progress and accomplishments. It is also time to begin visualizing your best-case scenario: achieving your vision. How will you feel? How will you celebrate? Who will be there for you from beginning to end?

You've probably heard the saying, "The journey of a thousand miles begins with a single step." Never has this been more true than in terms of achieving a major vision in your life. You must fight the tendency to become overwhelmed with all that must happen *before* you reach your goal. The simplest way to do this is to break it down into a series of small, even tiny, steps that move you closer and closer to your vision.

When you are able to see progress by completing many steps along the way, you can't help but be encouraged and grow in your belief that you *will* realize your vision. It may seem cumbersome to work through every step you must take to get to the end, but it is vitally necessary. Something happens when you think through and identify every incremental action that must occur for you to succeed. No longer does the magnitude of the goal seem beyond reach. Armed with a plan, you are empowered to move forward.

Whether you're pursuing a vision individually or as a team member or leader, there are certain criteria your benchmarks must meet if they are to provide the most benefit to you along the way. These criteria are frequently referred to as SMART goals, an acronym that will help you identify the most effective steps along the way.

This is what the acronym stands for:

S – specific, clearly-defined steps or actions

M – measurable, something against which your progress can be compared

A – attainable and challenging, but not out-of-reach

R – relative, don't add unnecessary actions or procedures, keep the main thing the main thing

T – time-bound; there must be a time limit to complete each action by or human nature would lead us to delay and procrastinate indefinitely

When you create SMART goals, you are establishing an environment of acceptance and accountability towards the actions you must take in order to achieve your vision. You have, in effect, established where you are wanting to go and what you are going to do to accomplish it, how you're going to do it, and by what date.

You are also setting the stage for success.

When I first started to write this book, I had so many ideas and so many stories I wanted to share, I did not know where to begin. My mind was on overload with all the considerations. Should I share that? Is this really helpful? Will this help people the most? And then I stepped back, took my own advice, and began asking myself a series of questions that would put me on the road to clearly defining my vision for the book and what I needed to do to make it happen.

These are just a few of the questions that helped cast the vision for this book:

» What type of book do I even want to write? Why?

» What kinds of research must I do to lend credibility to

what I am presenting?

» Who can give me honest feedback regarding my plans and progress along the way?

» What major leaders (CEOs, entrepreneurs, influencers) should I consult for their ideas and to test my ideas?

» How can I best encourage, motivate, and inspire those who read the book and follow my suggestions?

» What personal challenges and victories can I share to make my message more relative to my readers?

» How can I best engage my readers so that they want to continue reading?

Once you have asked and answered questions such as these that demand you clearly identify your vision, it's time to draft a timeline. Whether it's weeks or years in the process, make sure it is both attainable and reasonable based upon the complexity of your vision and the time you can commit to it. Remember not to set the bar for accomplishment so high you become discouraged. Lofty goals are admirable, but they must also be reasonable; otherwise you'll become discouraged early on and will quit. The same is true for the timeline you set—it must be intentional *and* attainable.

From here you are set up perfectly for the next step: visualization, or projecting upon yourself how it will feel once you realize your goal. Many, many successful business men and women are masters of visualization. They have come to appreciate the power behind this simple technique and use it to their advantage over those who don't.

Just as you first identified your vision and then the steps you would take to accomplish it, visualization takes it a step further—it develops the emotions tied to your vision. When you do this, you gain clarity to move forward and the motivation and excitement you'll need to tackle your detailed plan of action.

Here's all you do:

Sit down in a comfortable place or position. Clear your mind as much as possible and close your eyes. Now create a mental picture of what it looks like when you've realized your vision. Ask yourself questions such as these:

» How will my life be different? What areas will remain unaffected?

» Will there be a significant shift in the timeline of your life, as in a 'before' and 'after' obvious difference?

» How will my family and friends be impacted?

» Where will you go once you've reached this summit?

Because visualization is so powerful, it's no surprise that top tier athletes use it all the time. Most Olympic athletes have envisioned themselves on the podium receiving the gold medal and singing the national anthem as their flag is raised. If this simple process is so effective for Olympic athletes, why wouldn't we tap into it for *our* growth and achievement also?

A Personal Turn-out

I first learned the power of visualization from my dive coach in college. Even though I had never competed on any swim or dive team before, I thought a childhood of swimming and diving off the board at the neighborhood pool was certainly enough to earn me a spot on the team. After all, I could do a 1-1/2 flip off the board. What more could I possibly need to know?

Unbelievably, I made the team—but not as a swimmer. The coach was one short on the dive team and so I raised my hand, confident the flip and a half would serve me well. Imagine my surprise when I learned the bar was considerably higher in collegiate competition. I had to learn so many things. Dives and flips and twists. *And then combine them!* I had never done anything like this before! I was in, quite literally, way over my head. I soon learned form was crucial. So was the degree of difficulty. And so was entry into the water—the less splash, the better. I had never given any of these things any thought before; I just swam and dove because it was fun.

Fun left the building a few practices in as I was challenged to try a reverse dive. It certainly wasn't the most technically difficult dive I had ever tried; it was just scariest one. I was petrified I would hit my head on the board coming down.

That's when my coach introduced me to visualization. First, we watched films to see and understand what the proper form and technique looked like. Then, she would have me visualize and actually try to imagine what it would feel like to properly execute the dive. She took me through step-by-step of what it would take to do a reverse dive. She also had me envision waiting for the judges to award me a perfect 10 for my performance.

Even though I never actually received a perfect score, I gained something much more valuable—I felt confident and in control of my performance. I was able to put my fear aside, keep trying, and continually improve. Not surprisingly, this same process is important whether you're diving into a pool or just working through life.

It is my hope that by now, that if you've followed through on these first three steps—determining your type of vision, identifying the importance of your vision *to you,* and visualizing your expected outcome—you are even more motivated and passionate about accomplishing your vision than when you first started.

Progress is contagious. One small victory makes you want to tackle the next. Reaching a landmark level motivates you to stay on course. And looking back at how far you've come can inspire you to keep going when you want to take a break.

Stay the course, friend. You are getting closer.

Communicate Your Vision with Passion and Energy –

Now that your vision is clearly defined and you know what it will take of you, it is time to communicate your vision to others. If your success depends on the support of others (and spoiler alert—it *always* does) you must be able to effectively and convincingly share your passion, excitement, and motivation with them. Whether you're leading a team or pursuing an individual vision, you must present friends, family, and other potentially supportive individuals with the specifics of your vision. Share the details of what you intend to do. Explain your motivation for pursuing it. Tell them what you hope to accomplish when you reach your goal. In doing so, they will come to understand, and hopefully join you, in your journey.

Especially if you are leading a team that must work together in order to reach the vision, it is extremely important that your team members come to be as committed as you are. Otherwise, if you move ahead without the buy-in of those involved with and affected by, you are greatly diminishing your odds of success dramatically.

Spend some time making a list of those who could help you on this journey. Some may be onboard from the start, offering to help in any way possible; others may be of assistance for a time or season of your pursuit. Either way, make it a priority to identify who you think can best help you and where they might be most beneficial.

Before approaching anyone with your newfound vision, give considerable effort to preparing what is commonly referred to as your 'elevator speech'—a brief 1-2 minute summary of what you're striving for and why. Most times you will have a very small window of opportunity to gain someone's buy-in. Make the most of these precious seconds by being as prepared as possible.

I learned this the hard way on my first try-out for 'Survivor.' I had 60 seconds to differentiate myself from the thousands of other people the decision makers had seen that day. I didn't prepare and I failed. But I learned from it.

If you've ever watched 'Shark Tank,' you know that wannabe entrepreneurs have only minutes to convince a panel of potential investors why they should fund their invention. They must convey their passion, share the advantages of their product or service, and convince 'the sharks' of their worthiness to receiving the financial backing. Time after time, the winners are enthusiastic, high-energy personalities deeply committed to achieving their goals.

Watch them and take note. Then use these same tactics when you are given the opportunity to communicate *your* vision. The more you believe in your vision, the better prepared you will be when the opportunity presents itself to share it with others. The better prepared you are, the better you are able to sell the vision to others. And the better you can sell the vision, the greater your chance of gaining support and fulfilling your vision.

A Personal Turn-out

When my son was in high school and my daughters were in college, I was offered the opportunity to take an overseas assignment. I was extremely excited because I had always wanted to live overseas to gain the global experience and to learn from another culture. But, this would be a huge decision for the entire family.

My husband would have to quit his job and take a role in the company overseas; my son would have to leave high school, give up his friends and girlfriend; and my daughters, although in college, would not have us close by and only get to see us a couple of times in a year. This was big. This would have far-reaching fallout on my entire family.

I was extremely excited because it was something that I had set as a goal. We had all talked about the possibility over the years, but it's a whole lot easier to get on board with things you don't actually have to sacrifice for. When the opportunity did come, it was a shock to everyone. My first priority at the time was to consider all the things that would be necessary as a family to make this doable.

This meant a change of school for my son, well-planned visits for my daughters, different work for my husband, and expensive visits back home to see my mom and brother. What would we do with the house? How long would we be there? How long would we *want* to be there? The list of questions I had—*we all had*—was endless.

However, before I worked through all the specifics and logistics a move like this would entail, I knew one action item preceded them all: getting my family to feel the same excitement I felt and see all the potential benefits we could all gain from the experience. I thought about all the things that would be important to both my husband and son and wanted to be sure those things were taken care of first so that I could best show them my concern for them and their happiness. To be clear, I wasn't trying to manipulate them or the circumstances—actually quite the other way around—I wanted them to know they were the first priority.

In the end, my family was agreeable to the adventure. No guilt. No pressure. Just a better understanding of the opportunities such a move would bring with it. We stayed a year, soaked it all in, and took advantage of every adventure we could while there. I was able to fulfill a career-focused goal *and* my family had once-in-a-lifetime experiences—a win-win for us all.

Generally, however, when you are sharing your vision and hoping to bring others on board with you, the focus needs to be *on the audience.* It has to be about *their needs,* what *they will gain,* and how will *they* benefit, if they are to join you in this pursuit. If you make it about all about you, you'll miss the mark.

As you look at all the opportunities throughout your life, you must create your own pathway to success. You have to consider what you need to do to achieve your goals and what support you are going to need along the way. When you communicate your vision with passion, it creates excitement amongst your supporters and when they get excited, they become willing to help you achieve your vision.

Build a Movement of Inspired Champions –

As you're sharing your vision and gaining momentum, it's not just important to bring others along with you, it's vitally important to bring *the right people* alongside you. I call these people your inspired champions because they bring with them the same level (or close to it!) of commitment and excitement you have. Depending on the complexity of your vision, these champions can be all types of people and have roles of varying significance. For example, if my personal vision is to get fit, a supporter could be the neighbor who watches my kids while I exercise, a friend who commits to exercise with me and holds me accountable, or a spouse that throws out all the junk food in the house. They could all be considered my inspired champions because, even though they may not be fully committed to my vision (because it is a personal vision), they are fully committed to helping me achieve my vision.

If you are working in a team environment, the roles, requirements, and organizational structure of the champions is usually much more formal and defined. In these situations, team champions must maintain a specific skill set that contributes toward the vision. When you lead such a group, you must identify successful, credible, and flexible champions who can communicate effectively with others. From there, you empower them to lead others just as you have lead them. You set the example they are to follow.

In one of my roles as head of a learning and development team, I was responsible for collecting data on how my team was spending their time. I wanted to identify tasks that were time wasters and therefore, not contributing the outcomes of the department. My vision for the team was to improve internal customer satisfaction and achieve a score of 80% by freeing up the team to be more hands-on with the line organization. This was especially important because we had just gone through a systems conversion and the frontline associates were still struggling with the systems change.

I implemented a documentation process that all team members were asked to fill out weekly. I knew they would not be happy about this change because it meant accounting for all their time, all day long. It involved detailed accountability and an extra administrative assignment—neither of which most of us welcome with open arms.

But I thought this through before I introduced the assignment and I knew what I needed to do. I selected one of the team members that had a great reputation within the team—someone well-liked and respected and known to be very successful at whatever she did. If I got her onboard with the change first, she would become my first champion. In implementing the change first, she would set the tone for how this new task was received.

As my first champion became comfortable with the new process, I was able to communicate the change to the team, citing her as an example of someone who had completed the task successfully. My champion shared the benefits she had realized and committed to help fellow team members do the same as they adopted this new process. Her buy-in and support made all the difference in the world to my team. What could have been met with dread and displeasure was instead presented and received as an opportunity for my team to spend more time doing what they enjoyed most—helping others. Win-win—all around!

Picking your first, or first few, inspired champions is critical to your success. They must be able to help others get on board with change, new processes, and far-reaching vision. Some may even go so far as to offer ideas for how they can help. When this happens, you know you have inspired them and they should quickly become a valued member of your support team. It is this core group of people who will be the ones you can count on to move the vision forward day by day.

Great leaders give real thought to the values, ideas, and activities that they are most passionate about. A compelling vision can truly change the world. Staying invested for the long haul, however, can be extremely difficult—especially when hard times arrive. Push through the difficulty. Your vision is worth the effort.

To believe in yourself, your abilities, and your vision is one of the key secrets to your success. Commit yourself to meet your personal goals and hold yourself accountable *to you*. Create a vision that motivates you to remain committed. Your results will be evident in the actions you take, the values you hold, and the beliefs you profess. A compelling vision about which you are truly passionate will inspire you and others to:

Believe.
Commit.
Achieve.

A Moment to Reflect –

You now have the tools to identify, define, and implement your vision. Is your mind overwhelmed with ideas and possibilities and dreams? Are you ready to get started? Let me encourage you to dedicate a block of time to do some soul searching and reflect on yourself, your ideas, and your passion. Discover what motivates you. And in doing so, you will find your purpose.

The time to take action is *now.*

"'My people perished for lack of vision,'
the Bible tells us.

Being a leader means you must know where you
are going so others can follow.

Without clear vision and seeing the end game,
you will wander aimlessly."

–Mike Holloway
"Survivor" Winner, Season 30
San Juan del Sur, Nicaragua, "Worlds Apart"

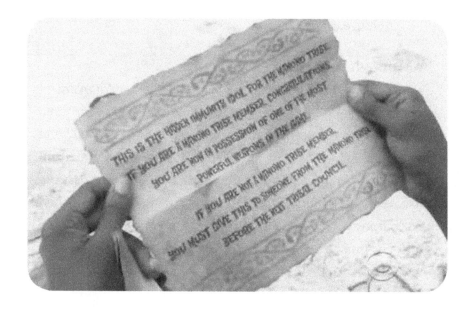

Hidden Clues on "Survivor" are important. People will want to follow you if you have a clue and you share it with them because you have their best interest at heart. Influence is successful when you are genuine and care about others.

Influence

I is for Influence

Let's start this discussion by defining what influence means in terms of leading others. Traditional definitions usually cite influence as the power to make someone or something change, move, or adapt. It can be overt and powerful or understated and subtle. It can be intentional or not, but it should never be forceful.

Intentional influence is a learned skill. It is also a powerful tool in the hands of an accomplished leader. I've often described influence as not just getting people to do what you want them to do but making them *want to do it*. When you are sharing your vision with others, you are *influencing others*. When you are relaying your passion to others, you are *influencing others*. Excitement becomes contagious and that's when influence happens.

People are just naturally more apt to follow someone they can believe in and someone who creates an emotional connection with them. The secret to understanding how to best influence others is simple: understand *their* motivation. This means you must uncover what is important to them, what are they passionate about, and what they want to accomplish. Understand this, and you will shape legions of people.

Most of us realize we will need the support of many others as we begin to pursue our visions. In fact, I would go so far as to say, *every vision requires the support of others; no one person can fulfill a vision on his or her own.* Think about it—we need the support of others *in virtually everything we do.* No matter how independent you consider yourself, we all rely on others to some extent and in some capacity throughout our lives—*especially when we are pursuing our vision.*

Leadership based upon integrity uses the power of leveraging influence among friends, family, co-workers, and even complete strangers, in an open and transparent manner and not based upon an ulterior motive or hidden agenda. As a leader, when you share your intentions and needs honestly, people will appreciate the vulnerability and information. They will feel valued and are much more likely to help as they are able. When you influence people this way, you set the example for them to follow *as they influence others.*

Before you go about the business of influencing others, it is helpful to identify who you respect. Ask yourself these questions:

» Who do I respect most? And why?

» What have they done to earn my respect?

» Is it what they do, what they've accomplished, what they've overcome, or all of it?

» Is it because of their notoriety or because they seek no audience at all?

» Have you seen them experience great success?

» Have you witnessed them dealing with defeat?

» Who is it you think influenced them to become who they are today?

» What is their backstory?

» What have they sacrificed along the way to achieve what is important to them?

» Do they consider it a wise trade-off or regret it?

» Can you adopt some of the traits and characteristics you admire in these people as your own?

Let me be clear on two specific points concerning influence:

Influence is not a bad thing; it can be, but used with integrity, it can be a tremendously positive tool to motivate, inspire, and encourage others well beyond what they consider to be limitations and obstacles.

Every effective leader is an effective influencer.

I believe there are four crucial elements to leading and influencing others with integrity: character, competence, commitment, and courage. When you have a good understanding of each of these traits, not only will your influence become more effective; it will also be recognized as honorable and worthy of others' following and respect.

Character –

Most of us have a general understanding of what character is—our values, beliefs, moral compass, or conscience that forms the basis for what we believe, how we act and speak and think, and the boundaries within which we live our lives. Character is who we are at our core.

You have to understand and strengthen your personal character before you can expect others to do so. People want to follow, connect with, and support those who exhibit a strong moral character and stand for things that resonate for the greater good. A consistent trait of people with good character is integrity. They don't necessarily do the right thing all the time (none of us do), but they rarely, if ever, waver in their commitment to their personal integrity. People with integrity are almost always valued and respected for their consistency of character, their ability to keep issues and conflicts in perspective, and their willingness to do the right thing over the easy thing.

For me, if I know and trust a person's character, I am automatically more receptive to what they have to say or ask of me because I am able to trust that they have my best interests in mind. When you bring someone with good character into the mix, it can change things dramatically because you know there are boundaries that won't be crossed, behaviors not tolerated, or excuses offered for actions taken.

A Personal Turn-out

Not too long ago, I was exposed to a boss with character flaws. *Serious, over-the-top character flaws.*

I was warned during my interview for the position that the boss was often very difficult to deal with. I was told that when he was good, he was great, but when he was stressed, he would become unreasonable. I thought I could handle it and thought it was worth the risk because I considered it to be the perfect job to advance my career at that time. I considered it more of a challenge at the time, telling myself there was nothing I couldn't deal with to make that happen.

I learned very quickly that this individual did not truly care about me and did not have my best interests in mind. When I took the job, I made it clear that I needed to be available during the month of October to watch my oldest daughter play her last year of soccer in college. Because the position was an overseas assignment, we made the agreement that I would work in the states for the entire month of October so I could go to her games on the weekends.

As we got closer and closer to October, I was told that I had so much to accomplish that I would only be able to be in the States for two weeks instead of the previously agreed upon four. I was livid. This broken trust meant I would no longer be able to watch my daughter play her last year of soccer in college. It was devastating to me because it was not something that I could ever see again.

Looking back, I probably should have seen the handwriting on the wall but I chose to overlook it because I loved the job so much and believed the assignment was exactly what I needed to round out my skillset. Except…this wasn't the last time my boss' lack of character spilled over to me and my family.

A few months later, all my family was scheduled to travel overseas to visit and be together for the holidays. My daughters were both in college, so I hadn't had the opportunity to see them in months. I was counting down the days until they arrived.

I had made arrangements to take the last week of the year off to spend it with my family. We planned and paid for a trip to an island and were all excited about the adventure. When I reminded my boss when I would be out of the office, mostly just as a courtesy, he told me taking the last week of the year wasn't a good idea and that I should consider canceling the trip. Again, this was despite the fact that I had cleared it with him well in advance of booking flights, reserving hotels, and making costly and already paid for plans. He was unmoved by my situation.

It was at that moment I realized the true character of my boss and came to understand a consistent pattern: he would say what I wanted to hear in the moment to appease me, make promises at the time, but later renege on them because they meant nothing to him at all.

I made the decision to go on vacation and spend the time with my family as planned. I was glad I did, and in the meantime, it had become painfully clear to me that working for someone who truly didn't care about me was going to be a problem. Before long, I began to see other signs revealing his true character as well. I accepted it and endured it until one final encounter pushed me too far. It was the last straw. And I let him know exactly how I felt about him.

It started out as a simple misunderstanding, but it didn't end that way.

I had allowed an employee to work from home because my boss was in town and expected to be in the office. Because ours wasn't his primary location, he didn't have a designated office or any workspace for that matter. We were full-to-overflowing and had no extra available space for him to work. This led me to asking an employee to work from home *just for the day* so that his office would be available for the boss.

Apparently, this wasn't an acceptable solution to my supervisor. In fact, he considered it stupid and irresponsible and told me so in no uncertain terms. He called me into the borrowed office and proceeded to lash out at me. I couldn't believe the level of his anger over one trusted employee being allowed to work from home in order *to accommodate him.*

I was so caught off guard by his overreactive response, I lost it. When he screamed at me, I screamed right back, even cursing him. Not surprisingly, it was absolutely the worst thing I could have ever done because I had allowed *his bad character to influence my good character.*

I can laugh about it now and even managed to learn some valuable lessons from our colorful discussion—cursing and all! After I calmed down, I made a mental note of a couple of key things I would never do: go back on my word and never treat anyone the way I had been treated. I also came to see the importance of maintaining good character *at all times.* My boss may have had positional power through his title, but his level of actual leadership and influence was almost nonexistent and completely out of line with how I influence others. My vision was, and continues to be, to lead others, respect their efforts, abilities, and contributions, and help them to be as successful as possible. That is the power of influence.

For most of us, how we are perceived by those we lead and how we see ourselves are two different viewpoints. We know our intentions and can easily justify our actions, but unless we clearly communicate this to our followers, we open the door to misunderstandings and confusion. But the solution is an easy fix: Ask. That's it. Ask for feedback and encourage complete honesty. *Not* asking for feedback is one of the biggest mistakes leaders can make.

To be sure, you must temper any feedback you receive with this simple understanding— everyone operates from a different set of values and beliefs. However, with a strong foundation of trust and an environment that encourages honest discussion, you can always find common ground to work from. When people trust your character and know you will treat their differences with respect, it removes the stigma of judgment and makes it so much easier to see the commonalities.

Good character is *the key* to opening doors and influencing people. In the end, your character speaks above all other leadership skills.

Competence –

Competence is directly linked to success for a couple reasons. The obvious one—the more educated and competent you are on a subject, the greater the opportunities that become available to you to succeed. Secondly, people are just more inclined to trust, follow, and listen to those they perceive as competent, no matter the subject. Most people are open to learning new things in areas they know little to nothing about. Competency brings with it the interest of others. Add to that a bit of confidence and persuasiveness, and you will be able to harness that interest and influence others towards believing in your vision.

Becoming competent, even in just one or two areas, is an ongoing process. You have to work towards complete understanding, possibly even mastery of a subject, and work to stay up-to-date on changes in your field of expertise. You also need to determine where your competencies currently lie and consider how they might best be applied when you set your goals for achieving your vision.

Consider coaching baseball for example. To begin with, you'd need to know the game backwards and forwards, the rules and regulations, and the best practices of successful coaches. From there, those above you will come to expect a winning record and you must establish a reputation for developing strong players. If you fail to do any of these, your competency will eventually come under question and your tenure as a coach will probably be short-lived.

In the business world, your competence can be judged on your skill, your understanding of the industry, your functional area of expertise, your reputation as a leader *or not,* and ultimately, results. To be blunt, competition in the business world is fierce. Competency is expected, not a value-added option.

When pursuing your vision, you need to have mastered competence in your general field and you must be able to clearly and articulately demonstrate that competence to others. Taken a step further, it will benefit you greatly if you have the forethought and ability to anticipate how others may test your competence. Think about a time when you were truly engaged in a topic that you knew little about. Did you ask follow-up questions? Did you question the statistics presented or the legitimacy of the facts cited? Of course, you did—and others will do the same *to you.*

As I mentioned previously, becoming competent and proficient at a skill or within a specific area is evolutionary but you must have at least a solid working knowledge of a subject before you set out to influence people toward your vision. When you do, you'll soon find that competence leads to credibility. People will listen to those that are credible and they will base their opinions and decisions on proven results.

A Personal Turn-out

On 'Survivor,' my tribe lost the first challenge which meant we had to win the next one or we would be faced with going to tribal council and voting out one of our teammates. We were already down one member and couldn't afford to lose another. As we were talking in the shelter and developing a strategy for the next challenge, one of the guys told me I had to sit out of the next challenge. But his reasoning was ridiculous *and offensive*. It wasn't because I was the weakest link—far from it—but because he was concerned about upsetting another team member. What? Was he crazy? Did he think I would willingly accept his directive? He obviously didn't know who he was dealing with.

I clearly had better athletic skills than the individual he was referring to, but again, my ability wasn't the issue. Between me and the other member, I was hands-down the logical choice to participate. Our discussion reached an impasse and I knew it would be up to me to influence the rest of my tribe by explaining what I could bring to the challenge.

I had to focus on my skillset and have the courage to bring it up if I wanted to participate. It took courage to speak of my competence but suffice it to say I did not sit this one out. In fact, I was able to contribute significantly to our tribe's effort in the challenge—*a challenge which we won.*

Commitment –

Let's assume you've given some serious thought to developing your vision. You've considered any and every opportunity available to you, discovered where your true passions and talents lie, and visualized what success looks like *to you.* From here you must narrow your focus to a single, achievable vision, taking time to factor in your current circumstances, the support system you currently have vs. the one you hope to have, time, money, and the other realities of life. You'll want to consider every facet of pursuing this vision based upon two priorities—your passion for the project and your ability to wholeheartedly commit to achieving it. Big visions bring with them big commitment—unyielding and absolute commitment.

I think as humans we are naturally curious and hopeful and easily excited by the new ideas that visions are born from. That's a great start—you should be curious and hopeful, but that's all it truly is—*a start.* Don't stop there. Many of us have pages of ideas, thoughts, wishes, and bucket list items. We'll get a new idea, run with it for a short while, and give up at the first hint of challenge or resistance. When that happens, remember this: No commitment = no vision.

Consider creating a vision board, a journal, or just a file of ongoing ideas. Don't toss them aside just because the timing isn't right. They may not be feasible now, but they could be great fodder for your next vision.

While your vision may evolve as you work to achieve it, there can be no question of your commitment to a single purpose. This is because people will only allow themselves to be influenced by you if they see and believe you are fully committed. You must be focused if you're asking the same of them.

Think about a time you were in a restaurant and you asked the server for a recommendation off the menu. Were you influenced by the server who said, "everything is great!" or were you more inclined to take his recommendation for a single dish because he had tried it and he spoke of it confidently? Probably the latter, right? He believed in it and convinced you to do so too.

When people perceive commitment and confidence in a recommendation, they are easily influenced because that confidence is transferred. I've worked with many leaders in the corporate world and have found that those who jump from one big thing to the next are usually the least successful. Their efforts are scattered, their teams are confused and unfocused, and their lack of commitment is obvious. Over time that behavior greatly diminishes their influence as leaders and visions are compromised.

When we remain committed, we are the most successful. It's exciting to be intrigued by 'the next best thing' and the potential it brings with it but remember this: every old innovation or invention or concept was once 'the next big thing.' So whether tried and true or new and exciting, reaching a vision only works when you do. And that means time, effort, and a staggering amount of commitment.

Commitment to a single vision helps keep you focused on the journey at hand. It helps you use your most valuable asset—your time—the most effectively rather than chasing unrelated and wasteful side goals. No matter your title, rank, or level of achievement, you're given the same 24 hours a day as everyone else—CEO or babysitter. Your challenge is to use it wisely. Commitment is what eventually landed me on 'Survivor.' Becoming a contestant was important to me, so I committed to stay at it *until I was selected.* Four years of applications and nine videos later I got the call I had been waiting for. I was selected because I had remained committed.

Leadership and commitment go hand in hand. One cannot exist without the other. And one develops the other. They simply cannot be separated. As Peter Drucker said, "Unless commitment is made, there are only promises and hopes... but no plans."

Courage –

I believe that every individual is capable of courage if put in a circumstance that speaks to their heart. Having courage can be risky. That's because, whether you must demonstrate great feats of courage or small ones to gain the influence you need, you must be willing to stand up for what you believe in. As the pioneer of your vision, people will follow your lead.

Despite the inevitable criticism and obstacles that will come your way, you have to have the courage to continue to move forward…toward your vision.

A Personal Turn-out

I was in a meeting with a team of high level executives at a large company I was working for at the time. We were tasked with implementing a process within the different offices to create more focus on our corporate goal. Even though I had been certified to deliver this process within the company, the executive in charge wanted to change the process *after* we had purchased the program. *After* my team had become certified on the process. And *after* we had all agreed on the rollout strategy.

In the meeting, he was the boss because of his positional power. He felt strongly one way and I was equally passionate about not changing the focus. We had agreed to the plan several times before that meeting. I wasn't sure what had changed his mind.

I presented my points *again*, adding that I felt very strongly that a change in process would diminish the effectiveness of the plan. I didn't do this because I wanted to be stubborn or win this battle; I did it because it was a proven certified process that had worked in many other companies. We discussed it further and he shared his ideas. He felt as strongly as I did. We both got a little heated and a little louder. We didn't cross the line to the point of arguing or offending each other, but we were both very passionate about our respective points of view.

In the end, we compromised and came to a solution that worked and was acceptable to us both. The program was rolled out and successfully provided some much-needed focus to our associates. Our relationship after that discussion grew closer because we had each listened to one another, both shared our ideas and explained why we felt so strongly about them, and because we both trusted one another to have the right intentions in mind. It wasn't about power in this case; it was about doing the right thing.

It can be risky going against your boss, but if you go about it respectfully and allow your intentions to be known, presumably that you are focused on the good of the team/organization and not your own personal 'win,' you can, indeed, influence others to see it from your perspective. Conflicts and challenges require courage. The people you lead will look to you to set the tone for how they are handled. People are more inclined to respect engaged leaders who admit fault, embrace criticism, and can also defend their ideas. Win, lose, or draw, life is full of situations that call for courage and an effective leader should be the first one to take the courageous path.

It also takes courage to build good character. It takes courage to become competent. And it takes courage to have commitment and gain the commitment of others. Courage is the underlying trait that helps you to influence others.

As a recap, the four personal characteristics you must have to influence people toward the success of your vision are: character, competence, commitment, and courage. Just as most of us are presented with daily opportunities to practice each of these traits, keep in mind that these are also the pursuits of a lifetime. One small victory in any of these areas makes it easier to achieve the others. These strengths build one upon the other as you handle the challenges that come your way with integrity.

The power and possibilities of influence are infinite—*truly infinite*. Remember that we previously explained influence as the power to make someone or something change, move, or adapt, either intentionally or otherwise. But, take note! You must understand influence should never bring with it malice, force, or corruption. In fact, it should be just the opposite.

Well-intentioned influence brings with it many benefits. First, it allows you to let go of all the worry and anxiety you might feel when faced with asking others to come alongside you. If you are truly passionate about what you are pursuing and share your true motives, you shouldn't feel guilty about sharing what you truly believe in. Second, when you influence people in a fair and transparent manner, they are bending to your will because they want to, not because they must. They are choosing to support you because they feel connected to and believe in what you are sharing with them.

Influence rooted in good has resulted in some of the world's greatest achievements. Think about the set-backs in modern history if someone hadn't influenced scientists toward the notion of space exploration or our founding fathers toward democracy or doctors toward cures for diseases. Recognize that influence should always be positive. In fact, when we are passionate and committed to a vision and use our influence to gain support, we are sometimes pushed to achieve more than we originally aspired to.

As I mentioned earlier, it is virtually impossible to achieve a vision without the support of others. Whether we need the substantial and unconditional support of many or just a small vote of confidence from a select few, we cannot do it all alone.

That's where influence comes in.

After you've described your vision with passion and energy, demonstrated competence and commitment, and asked for the support you need to make this vision a reality—what is it that keeps someone from saying "thanks, but no thanks" or wishing you well without joining your team?

Influence.

Influence leads casual encouragers to become sold-out supporters.

Influence leads supporters to become heartfelt believers.

Influence leads believers to support you, not just because *you* believe in your vision, but because *they* believe in it.

Sometimes, it can be difficult to get others to feel as passionate about a vision as we do. But since we consider it a vital part of our vision, it is a necessary step. Generating excitement, growing a following, and gaining the buy-in of others are all part of the process of influence and all require a willingness to learn about the character of the people you want to influence. Taking the time and making the effort to get to know what drives others can bring with it great and continual rewards in terms of gaining support. When you understand *their* motivation and see what is important to *them*, you are better able to show them how your idea *will help them* as well.

Influence is as much about selling yourself as it is about selling your idea. People are driven to success and charisma—especially when those qualities are coupled with a similar set of values. There are lots of ways to sell yourself, but the most effective way is the most authentic for you, one that reflects your natural style and manner. How you 'sell' yourself and your vision should complement what you stand for and what you have come to be known for as an individual.

One of the most effective ways I practice this is to ask myself the questions I would want asked if the roles were reversed. Questions such as:

» What exactly is your purpose?

» Why should I buy in to what you are telling me?

» What is in it for me? How will my life/career/happiness benefit from supporting you?

» What is required of *me* to become part of *your* vision?

Influence can change people's mindset and offer them insight into a perspective on ideas and processes and causes they might have never considered before. Many times, just this enlightenment excites them. However you go about it, *only you* know best how to present yourself and tell your story. Always keep in mind that we hold other's attention for only a short time and so it is imperative your presentation be brief and compelling if you hope to move the needle from just listening to all-out support.

Here are a few widely used practices that can help you best prepare your pitch –

Before You Get Started –

» Determine the steps you must accomplish to achieve your vision

» Determine who you need to influence and then do your homework *on them*
  • ask yourself why they should listen to you
  • understand their personality characteristics
  • find common ground between you and them
  • identify how *your* vision will benefit *them*

During the Discussion –

» Speak with competence and commitment
» Share the details of your vision
» Work to convey your excitement and compassion
» Show them why *their* involvement is critical to the vision's success
» Explain the benefits to them that will come of their support

I can't stress it enough—preparation is crucial. Think through every conceivable question someone might ask and have a ready answer. Any sign of hesitation or doubt can cost you dearly. It is also wise to prepare different ways to present the same information because everyone receives information differently. If you are prepared, you'll be able to switch gears to a different delivery technique that may resonate better with your listener.

And this—*this* is where so many drop the ball on 'sealing the deal'—don't forget to ask for what you want. *You will never get what you don't ask for.* Make sure you make 'the ask.'

A Personal Turn-out

Several years ago I was preparing for a meeting with a senior executive and his team to discuss their training plan for the year. Prior to the meeting, I was given the initial training budget and sales goals for the team. As I began to do my homework and identify their training needs, I realized there was a significant disconnect between the training budget and the skillsets required of the team members to meet their goals.

Knowing my client and understanding that success was paramount to his character, I developed an alternate training program along with the added cost that would allow them to achieve their business goals and objectives. I even went so far as to offer ways to measure success and overall effectiveness of the training program. I presented the team with all the options and made sure everyone involved understood this was not about increasing my budget for the sake of getting more money; this was about creating the right plan to support the needs of the organization. In the end, they believed in the benefit of the advanced training program and the direct impact it would have on results and decided to invest the extra money. It was a win-win for everyone but I was only able to offer alternatives because I was prepared!

Reflection

Influence is among the most powerful tools used by strong leaders. But before you begin focusing on others, give your own personal character an honest assessment. Are there changes you need to make? Are you committed to your vision and the actions that you need to take to make it happen? Are you competent to do all that is necessary or do you need to continue to learn and grow to gain credibility? Are you willing to put in the time and effort required to deliver your message effectively and create a team of inspired champions?

You must answer all these questions and more with a resounding 'YES!' before you go any further.

"I believe our lives are defined by our impact on others.

If I can help someone else grow, then they take a part of me with them.

In that way, I am my mother; I am my father. I am everyone who has shaped me, and everyone who has shaped them.

Your influence is more than your legacy.

It's your immortality."

–Adam Klein
"Survivor" Winner, Season 33
Mamanuca Islands, Fiji, "Millennials vs. Gen X"

Flint is important because everyone listens to the person who can make a fire. In the game of 'Survivor,' fire is your life and communication is a NON-NEGOTIABLE skill for VICTORY!

Communication

C is for Communication

In the spirit of effective communication, let's start this chapter by acknowledging what you've learned so far:

You know how to develop and define your vision

You understand the importance of influence to build a movement of inspired champions

The next step in the journey toward conquering your world is mastering the art of effective communication. If you can't tell others what you're pursuing, how you're going about it, and why you need their help, you're limited to only what you can do *alone*. And that brings with it limitations. Crippling limitations.

Most of us have messages coming at us from all directions all day long. Texts, emails, social media, radio, television, billboards, and more bombard us *all day, every day*. There is always someone trying to shout their message over the thousands of other messages we receive daily. Most of us are so barraged with communications, we find it's easier to tune them out and ignore *them all*.

The fallout of this never-ending stream of talk coming *at us* is that many of us have lost the ability to focus on the one type of communication that is the most important—personal communication. Ask yourself this–are you being communicated *with* or simply communicated *at*? That should tell you a lot about most of the messages you receive.

However, when you are working towards a vision, communication must become a 'two-way' give-and-take exchange. Otherwise, you simply blend into the noise of all the others talking 'at' people. It's a given that we all know how to communicate at least to some degree. The distinction is made between the uber-accomplished and the rest of the pack by how well the communication is shared *and received*. The importance of effective communication *about everything* cannot be understated.

Speaking from experience, ineffective communication can be the source of much frustration—whether you're giving it or receiving it. It wastes time, leaves people feeling confused or anxious, and most importantly, it makes them want to stop listening. As someone whose entire career has been based upon my ability to communicate, I have realized what I consider to be the underlying problem with most communication—we all think we are fabulous at it. After all, we know what we're trying to say. How hard can it be for someone else to interpret our words and understand our intentions?

Usually...*very difficult.*

Believe me, it is much harder than you think to have others understand precisely what you are trying to convey. Just ask most people what they consider to be the biggest problem in their marriages and the overwhelming majority will tell you it all comes back to communication.

Poor communication.

My husband and I are prime examples. We've been married for 30+ years and are still very happily married, but communication can still be a big deal for us. I can't tell you how many times I've had a conversation with my husband, and after listening for a few minutes, I have to stop him and ask him 'topic.' That's our signal that he's talking about something I don't know anything about and that he's veered off our original discussion into unknown territory with me. And he is someone I know very well!

He thinks he's shared the info with me before, but actually hasn't. We all do this. We all carry out a portion of vital communication in our minds without ever actually saying the words out loud. So when we jump into the details of something we haven't shared, everyone listening to us is confused. In our marriage, my husband and I have a comfortable rapport, so when we have these miscommunications, either one of us can call a quick time-out to get us back on the same page. In professional settings, it's not usually as easy to be that candid, especially when it concerns those above you not presenting the whole picture.

The second biggest problem with communication is that, because we are unique individuals, our minds simply don't work the same way as anyone else's. Each of us has had different life experiences that come together to shape our perceptions. These in turn lead us to receive and accept information differently. Some of us even have a 'trigger phrase' that immediately puts us either at ease in a conversation or on the defensive. You'll do yourself a favor to identify what those are for the people you communicate with regularly. And also for yourself.

For me, my negative trigger phrase is, "That won't work." That's all it takes and I'm off and running. If I make a statement and someone begins their response with "well, that won't work," I'm instantly annoyed. To me, if you are already jumping to a conclusion without hearing the full idea, it means that you are negating everything I am saying without giving me the opportunity to discuss it. Another one that makes me crazy is "I told you." I immediately think that person just wants to show how smart they are or imply I have forgotten something.

Triggers can damage a relationship, even unintentionally, if the perceptions and personal experiences of the listener get in the way. If you know what phrases 'push your button,' so to speak, you're better equipped not to overreact whenever you hear them. It's like taking a preemptive step *before* you lose your cool.

This is never more important than in working with people of different cultures. Many of the things you say and how you say them can be considered offensive and off putting to people from different parts of the country or the world. You know you mean well, but they don't.

A Personal Turn-out

I learned the vast difference between my meaning and other's perceived meaning through a presentation that went dreadfully wrong. Years ago as I was delivering a program to an executive team in China, I was explaining different ways to achieve the same result. I used what I thought to be an everyday phrase, "There is more than one way to skin a cat."

The gasps were audible and the horrified looks on their faces quickly told me my analogy did not translate well to their culture. They couldn't understand why I would ever want to skin a cat! Thankfully, I understood the whole communication process well enough to recognize something had gone terribly wrong. I quickly provided an alternate example that had less room for interpretation and we moved on. But, consider the possible fallout if I hadn't been paying attention to the visual cues of my listeners. Aside from thinking me a terrible person, the team would have left confused and unaware of the message I was giving them. The entire meaning would have been lost. I learned a valuable lesson that day—know your audience and actively participate in your own communication to others. Good communication is a two-way street and allows for feedback.

One-way communication is sometimes the only method possible but it has its own complications. When the listener is not allowed to ask any clarifying questions of the speaker, he/she is left to interpret the information as best they can and react accordingly.

There's an exercise that I perform when I'm working with teams in person. This exercise tests your basic ability to communicate effectively using only one-way communication. I begin by placing a jacket on the floor and asking for a volunteer to give me instructions on how to put it on. It always draws a few chuckles and smirks among my audience. Something we would all think to be an easy task is light years more difficult when only one-way communication is allowed.

Since putting on a jacket is such a simple and routine task, the speaker will often skip the most basic first steps such as "bend over and pick up the jacket." The participant must do EXACTLY as they are told—nothing more, nothing less. You can see how eye-opening this is when what we consider basic, simple instructions are overlooked. And that's not even taking into consideration the participant's perceptions or possible misunderstanding of the terminology the speaker uses. If you don't understand and can't ask for clarity, you'll likely get further confused and frustrated and nothing will be accomplished.

I love this exercise because it clearly demonstrates that we think we are being perfectly clear with our instructions, but we don't fully understand how the listener will digest the information. It's a great eye-opener that reinforces how vital clear and effective communication is to success. Try to do it yourself as a personal assessment and then share it with others who communicate with you regularly.

Now apply that same concept to understanding a new concept or process in the workspace that you know nothing about. If you can't ask questions, your job becomes exponentially more difficult. Outcomes suffer when communication fails.

The costs of one-way or missed communication within relationships and companies can be vast. Time is wasted, budgets are exceeded, and patience is worn thin all because someone didn't understand what was being said and couldn't or didn't ask questions. Sometimes we need clarity; other times more information. Still other times we need feedback or validation that what we are doing is what is asked of us.

As listeners, most of us assume we are the ones who didn't listen closely enough or were too distracted to fully grasp the speaker's intent. We blame ourselves and rather than stepping forward and asking for clarification or possibly risk being considered a fool, we remain silent and confused. I assure you, it is always better to take that risk and ask rather than moving ahead without understanding the full message.

A Personal Turn-out

I have worked with all different types of people throughout my entire career and it became evident after a few mishaps early on that some of my listeners considered it more of a priority to please me and *attempting* do as I asked rather than pushing for clarity about what I was asking of them.

I was living in Manila at the time, so there was already a significant culture difference between myself and my team of 12 direct reports. If ever there was a time for two-way communication, this was it. We were in a conference room discussing an upcoming project and I gave what I thought to be completely clear instructions for next steps. Imagine my surprise when I followed up with them a week later and nothing had been done. Not only that, I wasn't the only one surprised. My entire team looked at me in disbelief when they realized I had expected a totally different outcome.

Even though I had written in my notes exactly what I thought I had tasked the team with, no one truly understood what they were supposed to do and no one asked questions. Not a single person. In retrospect, I should have asked for clarification of their understanding or some sort of confirmation that everyone received the same message. Instead, I learned a wonderfully valuable lesson: adapt your approach to who you are communicating with, use other means of communicating if necessary (say it different, present it different, clarify it different), and verify your audience understands your message.

As a leader, you need to ensure that people understand what you are saying even when they choose not to ask questions. As a listener, you must ask questions whenever something becomes unclear or needs further explanation.

As much as possible, get to know your audience and their personality styles. When you know your audience, you can flex your communication style to better meet their needs. When you become proficient at understanding how your listeners process information, you will not only become a better communicator overall, but a better communicator *to them*.

Begin with learning what works best with your family and close friends. Try a few techniques and see what is most well received and what they respond to best. From there, concentrate on those you interact with most frequently in your career. Look for clues indicating real connection such as direct eye contact, a nod of agreement, and receptive body language. If your listener asks related follow-up questions, you can be sure they are hearing what you are saying.

There's a handful of ways people receive and process information, no one style better than the other. Some people do best with descriptive, well-chosen words. Others are more visually oriented and understand better when you paint them a verbal picture of your vision or challenge. If you're able to provide an actual picture, graph, or chart that illustrates your message, that almost always helps everyone 'see' the same thing you 'see.'

Most people communicate with others the way they like to be communicated with. We speak how we want to be spoken to. The upside of our individual style is that it comes naturally to us. We don't have to work too hard at it. It's what we know and what we practice. The downside with this approach is that it has the potential to alienate a good portion of the population, or rather everyone else who doesn't speak and listen as you do. With this in mind, it is critical that you gain the skills necessary to communicate in different styles and be able to read your audience.

Becoming a successful communicator isn't a difficult process. Virtually anyone can improve their skills but it does require that you continually and actively engage in the process of getting better. And the payoff? The payoff can help you to become more effective in *every* area of your life.

These are the four steps I teach for creating effective communication:

- » LISTEN!!
- » Develop the Message
- » Deliver the Message
- » Verify Understanding

Let me expand on each of these steps –

LISTEN! –

The first and most important skill required for successful communication is the ability to listen effectively. I get it—it sounds completely counterintuitive. How do you get your message across when you're the one *listening*? Trust me on this one—the only way to get your message across is to understand what resonates with your audience. You must position your message in such a way *they* understand what you are saying and that best captures *their* interest.

Understanding the art of listening is a skill everyone could use a crash course in. More than anything, it requires a consistent effort because we have become so inundated with so many messages coming at us. It is so easy to allow your mind to wander off and think of other things even when someone is speaking *directly to you.*

Our collective distraction is epidemic. We have become so conditioned to hearing the most urgent or the latest scoop or the most sensationalized, that we oftentimes miss what is right in front of us. Think about the last time you had a heated discussion. You *appeared* to be listening to the person. You nodded at appropriate times, even maybe made direct eye contact. You even *convinced yourself* you were listening.

But you probably *weren't*—at least fully.

See if this doesn't sound familiar regarding most of your day-to-day conversations: if you're not making a mental reminder about picking up the dry cleaning, you're probably thinking about where you're going for dinner or what you're doing next weekend. And if it's not personal details crowding your consciousness, you're almost assuredly thinking about *your response.* You're listening to respond, not to understand. You're focusing on *your* rebuttal, not on what the other person is saying.

But when you are proactively listening, you are listening to *understand* the viewpoint of the other person. Listening like this takes focus and patience and lots of intentional effort. If you are interested in the topic being discussed or you have a personal connection to the speaker, the focus is naturally easier. However, even in the best of these scenarios, our minds are still tempted to wander.

A classic example of this that always makes me laugh frequently shows up in movies. The guy is infatuated with the girl and, while she's fully engaged in the conversation between them, all he can focus on is how beautiful she is or how great her smile is or how good she smells. He looks like he's listening, but he'd be hard pressed to utter a complete sentence in response to all that she is saying. All the while, she thinks he's hanging on her every word because he seems to focused!

All too often, we start formulating our response within the first few seconds someone *else* starts speaking. We'll hear the first part of a sentence and start to tune out so that we can focus instead on how *we'll* reply rather than fully hear what *they* are saying. Worse yet, lots of us go so far as to finish the sentence *for them* with *our thoughts and not theirs.*

Much of this goes back to our desire to be efficient and anticipate what they're going to say. We want the bottom line. The Cliff Notes version. Tell me how this affects *me*, and let's move on. Force yourself to consider how you feel when others do this to you. Don't you want to grab them by the shoulders and say, "Hey listen! What I have to say is important!"? It's a common courtesy that has been drowned out by the 24/7 technology we've become accustomed to. It's also what I consider to be the cause of so many *avoidable* communication gaps.

In the name of bringing back a vanishing practice, I offer these suggestions:

First, realize that listening is both audible and visual. Sure, it is important to evaluate the words that are being spoken, but it is equally important to read body language and listen for tone. Only 35% of communication is verbal. That means the remaining 65% comes from nonverbal cues. People often say one thing and mean another but it is only by listening effectively and carefully observing that we can uncover their true meaning.

This is especially important to remember when you are the one doing the talking. Your mood at the moment, your authentic level of interest in the topic under discussion, or your like or dislike of those you are addressing can present body language inconsistent with your message. Say and portray what you mean to convey because others are watching you probably more than they are listening to you.

Develop the Message –

It takes much more time to craft a compelling and interesting presentation than people ever expect. Think back to what led you to create your vision in the first place and how you worked to narrow it down and keep it simple. If your message isn't perfectly defined and clear in your own mind, you certainly can't present it effectively to your listeners.

Just as developing your vision can sometimes be difficult, developing it into a clear and simple message can also be a bit of a challenge. We want to speed through the process and make it happen *now.* But thinking it through from the start will save you much time later and possibly even embarrassment or lost opportunities later on.

For example, say you lead an organization and you want to reinforce your company's core values, a large component of which is focused on customer service. Everybody knows what 'customer service' is. That's because everyone knows what 'customer service' means *to them.* What I consider important to customer service may not be what you consider important to customer service. The same holds true for *every single* person you ask. Everyone believes themselves to be right, *and they are!,* based upon what they value most.

And that's where the miscommunication comes in.

In the absence of a clear definition, we all default to *what we would consider* exceptional customer service—what seems obvious and logical *to us.* However, some of us may be very easy to please, maybe we tend to be overly compassionate, and are prone to write off the rude waiter as 'having a bad day.' We set the bar low and usually give everyone the benefit of the doubt. Extraordinary customer service is appreciated, but not expected.

Or maybe you're at the other end of the spectrum regarding what you consider excellent customer service. You expect and often demand your needs be met as part of the customer-provider contract. Prompt efficiency and a gracious spirit of service should be the minimum in your book.

Now consider what happens when these two expectations and temperaments come together to rate an establishment's customer service. You find yourself with satisfaction surveys all over the map—some ranting, some raving, and a whole lot somewhere in the middle. So what are you to do? Define it. Until everyone in your organization has the same definition of 'customer experience'—what it looks like, how it is best accomplished, and the limits to which they are allowed to go to please others, there will never be a consistent standard of service.

These same parameters apply when you get down to the specifics of defining your vision. There has to be a standard against which you are able to measure your effectiveness. Once you feel like you have a good handle on your message, test it out on several different people. When you have finished your delivery, ask them to repeat back exactly what they just heard. This is a great tactic used by large corporations when they are preparing to roll out a new idea or product. By testing your message with a variety of people and practicing your delivery, you become more and more comfortable in your delivery style as well as gain a better understanding of how others hear what you're saying.

Now think about the words you use at home with your family. I would venture to guess that most of us have either said or had said to us, "You have a bad attitude; you need to change it immediately." But who knows exactly *what* to change? Think about it—what exactly is it that needs to be changed? Tone? Stance? Volume? Maybe all three or maybe *none of these*. Just like customer service, attitude can mean one thing to you and something totally different to someone else.

It would be so much more helpful to offer a specific behavior to be corrected rather than something so vague as 'attitude.' If you tell someone to, "stop rolling your eyes at me and listen to what I have to say," they know what is expected of them. A simple and specific directive beats a vague command every time.

When you choose the right words—specific, simple, and concise words—you are able to minimize (if not eliminate) the possibility of confusion and dramatically increase the chances of others *hearing what you're saying*. Only then can you expect them to produce the results you are asking of them.

Deliver the Message –

Once you have developed a clear message, the next step in the communication process is to deliver it effectively. Whenever I am asked to speak publicly, I always write my message out to help me actually see my words and make sure I'm including relevant points and engaging stories. I review it and then I practice. I say it out loud in front of a mirror, in the car, and standing as if I were on stage. I time myself, make notes about my delivery, and highlight key words and phrases I want to be sure to include.

Once I'm comfortable with both my message and delivery I begin testing it on people, again asking them to repeat back to me what they heard me say. When I see a discrepancy, I make notes and ask questions to see what I need to further explain or elaborate on. Usually this means giving specific examples to help them understand exactly what I am saying.

There are a variety of communication styles to deliver your message, but the one that is correct *for you* is the one that connects with your audience and best aligns in the way *they* process information. I have two key takeaways for delivering your message effectively.

Know the Audience You Are Delivering To –

Certain personality styles can hear words and process them effectively and immediately while others need to take notes, review them later, and offer feedback after they've had time to process the big picture. Some people understand best when they see the actual words on paper and still others need a visual aid to capture their attention to fully understand your message.

I am someone who can hear information and process it right away. And if I don't understand something, my personality allows me to be the first person to ask a question and engage the group out loud until I fully understand. Admittedly, this is not everyone's personality and that's why it is important to pay close attention to those with more reserved personalities.

People like this tend not to engage directly in a conversation but to participate in their own style by listening to the conversation and questions of others. They are also more likely to engage in a follow-up meeting and share ideas after they've had time to digest the information. In my experience, people who take longer to process information are at somewhat of a disadvantage because it creates a perception that they aren't fully engaged in the conversation. I know this isn't necessarily true, but the perception remains and can sometimes hinder success in the long run. Still, there are some people who like to repeat out loud what you are saying before digesting it internally. It helps them take it all in at their speed.

There is no right or wrong way to process information, but it is your responsibility to understand how the people you work with most frequently process the information you are charged with sharing with them. You'll likely encounter employees with all types of different learning and processing styles. The better you become at being able to discern and recognize these styles, the better you will be able to speak more effectively to them. The best informed and most productive team members are those that hear and understand exactly what you are asking of them.

A Personal Turn-out

I was working in a large organization with a team of 10 direct reports. One of them was the type of person who didn't like surprises. This individual functioned best when she had time to understand and digest potential changes before they actually occurred. A little advance notice went a long way towards helping her adjust to changes.

But as anyone involved in the corporate world knows, change is frequent and perpetual. Few things remain the same for any length of time in our constantly changing global marketplace. Adapting is a necessary skill.

Still, I valued this employee and wanted to do all that I could to make an upcoming transition as smooth as possible for her. I understood her most receptive communication style and I altered my approach to meet her needs. I also realized she needed just a little extra time to get on board and digest upcoming change. When a big announcement was coming out, I would meet with her the night before a major announcement even though I wasn't supposed to communicate anything until the following morning. I trusted her and followed this process several times because it was important to me to recognize her needs as much as possible. When it was time to make the announcement the following day, I would call a meeting and communicate the changes to everyone at once and we were all best equipped to move forward from there.

On another occasion I came to understand how personal perception can lead to friction. Again, I was working with a group of people and one of the executives shared with me a particular frustration. He mentioned that someone on his executive team did not participate in the meetings or bring any added value to the discussion. I listened closely to his comments so that I could best understand what the executive was looking to happen.

What I came to realize is that they had very different communication styles. The senior executive was a think out-loud person, meaning that he could easily share his ideas and thoughts out loud as he processed them. The other executive was a digest-it-and-respond-later person. Once I enlightened each of them on the communication style difference of the other, they were able to discuss things openly. This improved their communication process immensely.

Just as people are different and require different things to perform at their best, communication styles are just another aspect of effective communication worth taking into consideration. I have a husband and three kids. I can't communicate the exact same way to all of them because they are all different. They each have their own style of listening and it's up to me to speak to each of them in the manner that suits them best. It's like this with my family and friends and coworkers. You have to *speak how others best hear.*

The reason why most communication fails is due to the delivery process. If we don't put in the time to get to know our audience, they will only hear and understand part of what we have to say and that serves no one any good.

Nail the Delivery –

Many of us think through conversations in our mind and when we speak the words in our minds, everything flows nicely. There are no awkward pauses, we don't overuse 'um,' and we speak in a consistent rhythm, not too fast or too slow. But something happens when we actually *say the words out loud.* We lose our train of thought and get off track. We ad lib when the right word doesn't come to us. And we usually speed up because we want this train wreck to be over! Try making your presentation only in your mind and then again, out loud. I predict you'll be amazed at the difference between the two.

As we mentioned in the attitude example previously, clear and direct words, those not open to interpretation, are the most effective gift you can give your listeners. There is an old adage that states something to the effect of, *"I didn't have the time to write two paragraphs, so I wrote two pages instead.*" It's funny, but true and it applies to writing and speaking.

As you think through what you need to say, make every effort to say it as simply and concise as possible. Try avoiding using terms like 'that should' or 'that might' or 'let's try.' Those phrases are wishy washy. They give you a way out. If you aren't confident in your message, you won't get the champions to be confident either. Be direct and clear. If part of your message is to assign action, do so directly and address the person by name. If you want to nail your delivery, use specific words and provide examples that leave nothing to misunderstanding.

Suffice it to say, I've had to learn this first-hand. I was setting up a meeting with a business partner and asked, "When are you available?" She replied, "I have nothing until 6 p.m." I took that to mean she was free the entire day *until 6 p.m.* and scheduled a meeting at 4 p.m. for myself, a client, and her.

When I went to confirm our meeting about 30 minutes before the start time, she told me she wasn't available. When I reminded her that she said she was available until 6 p.m., she kindly corrected me. "No, go back and read what I wrote: I said 'I have nothing until 6 p.m.'" What she meant was that she had *no availability until 6 p.m.* We saw the exact same words and yet we managed to interpret them, not just differently, but *completely opposite,* from one another.

We could have been frustrated, but instead chose to laugh about it. When there are bigger issues at stake, it is imperative to go overboard in making sure what you are saying is what others are hearing and meaning.

Visual Aids –

If you choose to use a visual aid such as a photo or video, make sure you present it in the proper context. I usually prefer a visual component in my presentations because it helps to bring emotion into the message. I've used this technique often, but there was one time in particular when I was having a hard time getting my point across to a sales team that was trying to identify the barriers of increasing their sales.

Recognizing that my words weren't doing the trick, I walked to the flip chart and created a drawing of our business as a balloon right in the middle of the page. I added little people all over the balloon and identified them as our competitors—bouncing off our presence and trying desperately to cling to our momentum as we were rolling down the hill. This visual (albeit crude and on-the-fly) was just what some of the sales professionals needed to truly understand the vast market share available to us. From that point on, we were better able to realistically increase sales goals for the team.

Most companies and individuals rely on verbal communication to get their messages across. But don't be afraid to use additional, alternate methods of creating *and holding* your listeners' interest. Visual aids are especially helpful when you are talking about process improvements. It is also very effective to walk through a process, stop at each step in the process, point to it, and ask for feedback. In doing this, you allow everyone to think about the same step at the same time and bring their collective focus to one thing at a time.

Even if you develop your message perfectly and deliver it clearly and succinctly, it is *still* hard to hold the attention of a group for more than a few minutes at a time. At any given moment, there are several members of your audience who are thinking about something else for a few seconds. You must repeat the cornerstones of your message over and over in a consistent manner to make sure the most people have the best opportunity to hear it.

I have always heard of and believed in the 'Rule of Seven' which says a listener needs to hear something seven times for it to really stick. That also means you need to say it seven times to make that possible. Don't get caught up in the actual number of times you say something but work to repeat your key points several times over. Remember, just because you said your main point once, and you understand it, most people aren't going to remember it if that's the only time you say it. Repeat, repeat, and repeat your key points again and again and be consistent every time you deliver it.

If you say things with a different tone or different emphasis, your audience will not make the connection to hearing the same things differently. It's like re-watching a favorite movie a second or third time—sure, you know the gist of it, but every time you watch it, you notice or remember something different because your mind can't pay attention to every detail all the time. For this reason and all those listed above, to become the most effective communicator you can be, you must utilize all communication tips, tricks, and techniques you can to get your best message across.

Verify Understanding –

Even though this is the final step in the process, verifying understanding is a very critical step to ensure that everyone hears the same thing. The verification process is quick, easy, and fundamental for success. You simply ask the other person to share with you their understanding of your conversation—the goal, their individual call to action, and the timeframe within which everything is to occur.

When you ask others, encourage them to use their own words and not to read from their notes. This allows them (and you) to know what parts of your conversation really stuck and where there is still some grey area. This also allows the listener to share their ideas with you and ask questions in an inviting atmosphere. You can hear their perceptions out loud and understand if there is a disconnect between what was said and what was heard and you can clear it up immediately so that you both feel confident you are in sync. No matter your profession, whether you are in sales, service, operations, or just talking with your loved ones, verifying that you've heard the same conversation is paramount to communication.

Don't rush through speaking, especially when you're giving assignments or sharing major news, without pausing to verify everyone understands their role and the greater project as well. It's tempting to move on to the next order of business but pausing to ask for verification can save you endless frustration and time. It is much less time consuming to spend 15 minutes at the end of your meeting to verify understanding than to reconvene two weeks down the road after the train has gone off the track. If you want to save time in the long run, you must do this every single time you present. And remember— people may be hesitant to ask questions, so it is YOUR responsibility to check for understanding if you want a consistent communication process.

I don't believe the art of communication is ever truly mastered; it just simply can't be. It requires constant effort and attention and the honing of your skills. However, since I believe good communication is the most important skill a person can have, this lifelong pursuit will always prove worthy of your time as it allows you to develop relationships, build trust, and understand the world around you at a deeper level.

What more could any of us want?

"The art of communication is the language of leadership."

– James Humes

Reflection–

Now it's time to examine your communication style and discover what you can do better to adapt to audiences and present most effectively. These questions are a good starting point for your self-audit:

- » Are you a good listener?
- » Do you truly value your conversations with others and want to learn from them?
- » Are you focused solely on your own message and not paying attention to how others receive it?
- » Where can you improve your style?

"To be a good LEADER, one must be willing to FOLLOW good advice.

Sometimes people are too strong-willed and won't listen or heed words of wisdom from others.

I enjoy hearing HOW people got to where they are and what I can learn from their experience."

–Tina Wesson
"Survivor" Winner, Season 2
Australian Outback, "All Stars, Blood vs. Water"

My "Survivor" buff that can also be used as a blindfold. You will go blindly with people you trust. Your personal brand is built on trust.

T is for Trust

Trust is the basis for *all* relationships. In friendships, marriages, and professional relationships, if there is no trust, there can never really be anything beyond surface-level connections. If we are to have deep and meaningful personal relationships and strong, long-term, and productive professional relationships, we must prove ourselves worth of other's trust.

But have you ever stopped to consider how trust is built? How one friend becomes trustworthy and another not? Or how one supervisor is trusted and respected while his peers are not considered so? It's because trust is based upon what we say and what we do and whether the two align with one another *consistently* and over time.

That means this trust gig is not a one-and-done sort of thing. Especially in the workplace, your actions are *always* on display. And the one thing people most look for in deciding whether you're trustworthy *or not* is the consistency of how you speak and act. That can be an eye-opening realization if you allow yourself to fully consider how all-encompassing that is. Every day. Every moment. Every situation.

But by chapter's end, I'm confident you'll be better prepared to earn and maintain the trust of those most important in your personal and professional life.

Two Types of Trust –

I believe there are two different types of trust that make up most of our daily lives–situational and personal. Both are important to practice and both bring with them long-term benefits.

Situational Trust

We engage in situational trust interactions every day, oftentimes with strangers. For example, I trust the driver of the car next to me will stay in his lane. I trust that the cook working the drive-through won't spit in my food. I trust that a clerk won't steal my credit card number when I pay for something. These are non-personal trust interactions based solely on a specific need (i.e. I need to get to work, the cook needs to keep their job, etc.), and simply can't be avoided if we want to live our daily lives. While it is important to acknowledge that we engage in these types of trust interactions, they won't be our focus here because so many of them are out of our control. We can respond or react when someone breaks this kind of trust (i.e. crossing into our lane of traffic, stealing our credit card information, etc.), but much of the time we can't prevent it.

Personal trust

For our purposes here, we will focus primarily upon personal trust—the key ingredient for building strong relationships throughout life. In fact, if you get right down to it, personal relationships—one person to another—are really the foundation of our society.

Communities are formed, corporations are built, and families are created all based upon trusting relationships. Whatever your role in life currently—professional team leader or personal family manager, building and maintaining trust is paramount to being effective in your life. Just as we talked earlier about how none of us can reach our goals without the buy-in of others into our vision, it is imperative to understand none of it happens without trust.

As a leader and as a human, trust is essential. Trust is difficult to earn and takes time to build, but it can be easily lost in a split second based on your actions. In terms of leadership, people tend to trust those with the similar values and ideas as their own. They look for those they admire and those with a successful track record in challenging times. And then, even if you have a superb vision, a well thought out plan for making it happen, and execute it flawlessly, you still must earn the trust of those you consider your inspired champions to be most effective.

Trust is a non-negotiable and necessary characteristic to positively influence people. It doesn't automatically accompany a title or position. Nor should it. Trust is powerful and can compel people to put their hearts, careers, and reputations on the line for others. Trust can even mean the difference between life and death in extreme situations such as military operations.

It should never be taken for granted and should be consistently evident in how you speak and act.

Building trust within a company, team, or a community takes consistent dedication. Just as I shared how 'customer service' means different things to different people, trust also means different things to different people based upon their life's experiences, belief system, and personality type. That said, the most effective way to gain the trust of those you work with— *however they define trust*—is to consistently make sure your words and actions align with one another.

To assess your current 'trust-worthy' skills, focus on your real self and take an honest look inward. Be truthful with yourself and reflect on situations where you successfully built trust with others as well as those where you fell short and trust was revoked. It can be hard; it can also be life-changing.

A Personal Turn-out

There was a time years ago when I fell short of deserving the trust of my team. I certainly didn't intend for it to happen, but the situation evolved that way nonetheless. I loved being the woman in charge and was addicted to the power and control that came with it. At the time, I wanted to build my team into an empire organization with me at the top. Naturally that meant I wanted to keep adding staff. I felt that the sheer size of my organization would speak to my success.

As a result, I focused my time and energy on building a larger and larger team. When I had reached close to 250 people in my organization, it became painfully evident that I was more committed to myself than the team I'd worked so hard to accumulate. I recognized it and my team members most certainly recognized it. They could see I was more inwardly focused instead of working to create the vision and strategy they needed.

Their trust in me had diminished greatly and I knew I needed to correct it immediately through whatever means necessary. It was an uphill battle because so many had lost their trust in me. They felt abandoned and hurt. It was a humbling experience for me and one that I could have avoided if I hadn't allowed myself to be so consumed with status and power. I had quit looking out for those I was responsible for leading and had bought into the lie that the size of an organization mattered more. I was sorely mistaken.

I eventually left that company and began the process of rebuilding the relationships that I had hurt with my selfishness. It was not easy for me to look at myself and determine where I went wrong. My first reaction was to blame everyone else for the breakdown. But they weren't the problem. I was. I had to stop and look at myself in the mirror and determine what was truly important to me. Then I had to get to work on myself and learn to grow and develop my leadership skills that *focused on others*, and not myself. After years of repair, I was able to talk to many of the people on my former team I had hurt and apologize. It was a long time coming, but it was a turning point in my life and my leadership skills.

Being truthful with yourself is a necessary first step. You have to identify where you went wrong and what it takes to do better next time. It may be a matter of focus or priorities or misconceptions *or all of these.* But whatever the reason for your misstep, you always have the power to improve going forward.

Think about someone who you trust with your life—not someone you trust *in your life,* someone you trust *with your life.* Obviously, your life is of supreme importance to you so ask yourself why you trust them. What did they do to earn such sacred trust? Conversely, think of a time when you were unable to trust someone. What caused your concern? What made you distrust them? What actions did they do or not do? Once you have recognized these behaviors that have so personally affected you, you can begin to dissect *your* approach to building trust going forward.

What Works and What Doesn't When it Comes to Building Trust –

What Works

The basis for building trust can be summed up into three simple practices —honesty, open communication, and consistency. All are critical components of building trust. And they must all be practiced *all the time*. Your daily actions create your personal brand—who and what you become known for. If you don't operate the same way every day, people will take note of your inconsistencies and begin to lose trust in you. Believe me, it is much harder to regain people's trust once you've broken it than it is to win them over the first time. Sometimes it is even impossible. Value the trust placed in you and prove worthy of it every chance you get.

What Doesn't Work

Time after time I have come to see three primary behaviors that lead to the breakdown of trust between parties. It is the wise leader who takes note of these vulnerable areas and consciously works to avoid them at all cost.

Exaggeration and Lies

Exaggerating, lying, withholding information, and not keeping confidences are absolute deal killers to gaining trust. And the reason is simple: most people assume if you are willing to exaggerate or lie or not tell the whole story or even break a confidence in one instance, you are highly likely to do so again. And again. And when it might concern them next time. Or maybe it means everything you've said and done prior to this point has been based upon exaggerations, lies, or 'other versions' of the truth. When you give in to any of these destructive behaviors, you're harming your *past* reputation and severely limiting your trustworthiness in the *future*. It is much easier to get caught IN a lie than to prove you aren't lying *again* once you've lost trust.

A Personal Turn-out

In one of my former positions, I was working in a corporate training department and had to frequently review confidential department information. I needed a little help on some reports and chose to give access to one of my employees. Mind you, the information in these reports was strictly confidential and never to be discussed with any other individuals--within the company or otherwise.

Unfortunately, it came to my attention that my employee had shared a bit of what she had seen—*highly confidential data*—with another employee. I didn't know if this was the first time she had done so or the tenth, but it didn't matter. From that moment on, my trust in her was immediately and permanently broken. She never had access to confidential data again and she never had my trust again. There was *nothing* she could ever do to regain my trust because of the nature of what she shared. One bad decision on her part and all trust was gone.

Failure to Listen

We talked about listening a great deal in the communication chapter, so by now you can appreciate that failing to listen pushes people away. When we fail to listen, we are engaging in one-way communication. It is not effective and shows disrespect to the person speaking.

We are all communicative beings and we all want to be heard, but this works both ways—for the speaker and the listener. Have you ever been in a conversation with someone who goes on and on, to the point where you realize you're not even necessary. The person speaking isn't looking for feedback; they simply want a face to 'talk at.'

When you're the speaker, you lose people's trust when you take advantage of their attention and interest in what you're saying if you never pause to engage them. As a listener, it's also important to recognize the power that comes with your trust and to share it only with those who place a value on your thoughts and opinions.

Frequently, unprepared or ineffective leaders depend upon the expectation of trust as a means of explaining their failure to listen. They'll mention time is short, there's lots to be done, maybe other meetings to attend, and instead of asking for opinions or input about how to do something, they move directly on to making assignments and establishing responsibilities. They blame a time constraint, but what they're telling their team is 'trust me' or 'just do what I say' to honor the time crunch and not their trust. Clearly, these situations aren't ideal, but if you communicate your intentions up-front and explain that this isn't your typical method of communication, a loss of trust can be avoided. However, you should understand this is a risky tactic and these situations must occur sparingly. If a pattern of rushed behavior and lack of communication is identified, it will be treated the same as if you outright told your team members you didn't respect their opinions. That's a brutal reality, but that's exactly what your repeated behavior 'says' to them.

As you lead more and more people, it really is in your best interest to accept other people's opinions and give them the respect of considering their suggestions. When you make unilateral decisions, you aren't utilizing the resources available to you that are *intended to be used*—namely, *your people.* You're also not learning or growing, and most importantly, not gaining the trust of anyone—*except yourself.*

One thing many people fail to realize is that when you are giving directives without asking for and receiving the input of those most directly responsible, you become the one 100% responsible to blame if something goes badly. It also removes any buy-in from your team members. It's not their project; *it's your project*. They see themselves as simply a means to an end for you. Without any personal investment into a project, people are much more likely to take short cuts because it's not their job or reputation on the line; *it's yours*. Sadly, this set-up can even occasionally lead the more calculating among your crew to go so far as to even take action to ensure you fail. Everyone loses in this scenario. No trust is gained and no relationships are strengthened.

On the flip side, if you have solid, two-way communication with your team members or loved ones, you're much more likely to have strong relationships. When this is the case, you have the opportunity to work together to resolve situations *before* they become an issue and build trust in the process. Good relationships are the foundation of trusting, engaged, honest, and happy people. They're also the hallmark of successful people.

Lack of Accountability

Not holding yourself accountable for your actions is a sure way to eliminate trust. Most of us are prone to judge ourselves based upon *our intentions* and judge others based upon *their actions*. Sometimes there's a big gap between the two and without others providing some level of accountability, you're the only one against which you judge yourself—and that is a recipe for disaster.

Much of the accountability issue for leaders ties back to commitment. If you live by the old adage , 'your word is your bond,' you'll sidestep lots of potential problems. Otherwise, if you commit to something and don't follow through, or do it half way, others will likely lose trust in you. If you are unsure about your ability to meet a commitment, just don't commit. It is far better not to commit and save your reputation than to overextend yourself, not follow-through, and cause others to question their trust in you. It is always better to deliver on your commitment to a few than to disappoint many.

Here's a great example –Assume you're a salesman who just closed a whopper of a sale. Being the good salesman that you are, you tell the buyers you will follow-up in a week to make sure they are completely satisfied with their purchase. By saying you will personally follow up, you transform this interaction from situational trust to personal trust. You are stepping out from behind the curtain of transactional sales and into the space of personal trust. Now that you've done so, what is the perception if you don't follow up? Maybe nothing; or maybe the next time your customer chooses a different salesman. But if you honor your commitment to follow-up, you greatly increase the odds of creating a long-term customer.

And one other scenario – Let's say you are the person in charge of verifying facts before articles get published in a newspaper. Your reputation is impeccable and you are the 'go-to' fact checker trusted implicitly by all. Deadlines being what they are, one day you find yourself in a mad rush to sign-off on some copy and don't have time to fact check one small piece of data.

Rather than being accountable and communicating your situation, you take a short cut and send the article on *unchecked*. Once published, you learn the article was inaccurate; the one fact you didn't confirm was wrong after all. Your only honorable choice is to hold yourself accountable and admit to the mistake. Even if you make the case that it was *just this one time,* your reputation and the trust of the staff could be drastically compromised. Even though others may want to believe it was an isolated incident, they now have reason to doubt your integrity on past assignments and future ones, too. Beyond all this, even your many committed years of flawless service will forever be tainted. Still, accept the responsibility. Be accountable and apologize to all those affected. It is your only option on the road back to restoring your credibility.

On a more personal level, give some serious thought to the relationships most important in your life. Just as it works in professional relationships, if a loved one consistently fails to honor a commitment, you can't help but lose trust in them. You want to believe they will make good on their word and hold themselves accountable, but their repeated actions say otherwise. With no accountability in place for actually doing what they commit to, there's little reason to believe they will do so the next time they promise to do something.

Consistency is the antidote to unaccountability. When you have broken a trust, it is crucial that you remain consistently above reproach in your actions and words for an extended period. Only then will you prove you are worthy again of someone's trust.

Consistency earns trust and trust leads to loyalty. Trust is like a bank account for your soul. Every action you take and every word you say makes a deposit or a withdrawal. The deposits tend to come in slowly but the withdrawals can leave much more quickly. Monitor your words and actions in such a way that your trust account can support your style of living.

Reflection –

Reflect on the personal qualities that resonate with who you give your trust to. When you see these admirable traits in others and how you are drawn to and impacted by them, you can begin to incorporate them into your life as well. This also applies if you've ever revoked your trust from someone. What was it that caused you to do so? Was it a specific action or demeanor that you just couldn't get past? Ask yourself if you've ever been guilty of these same behaviors.

"Trust is based on how closely your actions align with your words.

It takes years to build and seconds to lose."

–Carolyn J. Rivera

"The gift of being a leader in the game of "Survivor" is tricky.

There comes a time when you want people to know that you have made proper moves and you want them to know that you've had your finger on the pulse of the game.

Doing that too early can lead to your untimely demise.

You also don't want to rule with an iron fist, as that not only puts a big target on your back, but it also makes you unlikeable.

Likeability is a major factor because of the social component of the game.

So, there is an art to finding the right balance between leading at the right times and applying the right pressure.

My game was predicated on leading challenges through action, not barking orders, while connecting with my cast mates on a personal level around camp."

–Wendell Holland
"Survivor" Winner, Season 36
Mamanuca Islands, Fiji, "Ghost Island"

Combinations are in so many challenges
on 'Survivor.' You have to find the right
combination that opens the doors to success.
You must have an open mind to see all
the options available to you.

Open Mindedness

O is for Open Mindedness

So far, the focus has been on the art of influence, the importance of effective communication, and the skills you must have to build and maintain trust—all crucial elements to fulfilling your vision. But there's another significant factor involved that almost seems counterintuitive to these—open-mindedness.

As a general population, I think we all want to believe we are flexible and open minded. We believe practicing open mindedness is a 'good thing' and we admit it's a part of learning and growing, both personally and professionally. But the fact is, we naturally tend to gravitate toward people and ideas that we already understand and that are in line with our basic values. We may give a few new concepts a fleeting consideration in an effort to appear open minded, but if we are truly honest with ourselves, most of the time we know we're just going through the motions so that we *appear* to have an open mind.

It is human nature to stick with ideas, concepts, and activities that we understand and bring us comfort. It is also human nature to lean toward the path of less resistance. All of us do so just by default. But if we are to become genuinely open minded, we have to do so intentionally.

I think most of us take a situational approach to open mindedness based on simple everyday decisions that don't really influence much change. Most of us would be open to trying a new restaurant at the suggestion of someone else. We might even listen to someone with a vastly different political opinion at a cocktail party. Or really live on the edge and try a new kind of running shoes. But none of this is *really* substantial evidence of living with an open mind.

Most of us like the idea of being considered open minded because it's usually thought of admirably. In times of struggle, we'll tell ourselves to be open minded as a means of coping with a situation we have no control over. It gives us comfort because we can't affect the possible outcomes. Just as importantly, when we are trying to influence others, we encourage and remind them to have an open mind as we share ideas that may seem far-fetched in the beginning because we want them to fully hear us out before forming an opinion.

The kind of open mindedness I'm referring to is the kind that will make a difference in your life—*true open mindedness.* Becoming and remaining open minded is an art that takes a concerted effort. But if you are diligent, this state of mind can eventually weave itself into your being and become second nature.

The state of open mindedness we should strive to achieve is holistic, and once mastered, automatically becomes part of your being and how you approach life. The true concept of open mindedness encompasses your mind, body, and spirit. It requires flexibility and change, as well as curiosity and excitement for things that you have not yet considered possible in your own mind. It is the truest form of adventure. By releasing the restrictions you've placed on your own mind and thoughts, you become capable of considering everything.

I'm not promoting all-out acceptance of any and everything by any means—certainly nothing risky or dangerous or that is in direct conflict with your core beliefs. But I do think you should give some merit to the unconventional or off-the-wall thoughts and ideas that randomly pop into your head and those that are communicated to you by others. That was certainly the case when I pitched my family on the benefits of moving to the Philippines.

The adventure comes in not knowing what to *always* expect. History and inventions are proof enough that some of the best things in the world have been attributed to an atypical mindset or different ways of approaching a longstanding thought process or problem. Flexibility is frequently the key that leads to innovation, advancement, and diversity.

When we repeatedly surround ourselves with people who look, act, and believe just like us, we limit our ability to be exposed to new and different ideas of thought. What we consider to be a safe circle of comfort actually keeps us from engaging with people who don't think like us and who have different viewpoints and priorities. This is especially true when politics or religion are being discussed. We think *how we see* these two controversial area is *the right way.*

Think about the last argument you had. Did you pause and give a second thought to their point of view? Or, as they were speaking were you already planning your response and not listening to them at all? Remember, this is where communication *ends* if both parties are unwilling to fully listen and respect the other person's right to their own perspective. This is also when relationships can suffer the most damage. When we allow our need 'to be right' to take priority over the consideration of someone else's opinion, we become inflexible.

Thankfully, there is a solution to this problem if you are willing to embrace it and retrain your brain towards perpetual open mindedness. For those of us who are 'big kickers' and continually reach for the stars, we must begin by admitting and accepting that we don't know *everything*, and that is okay. No one can experience and understand every possible situation, every perspective, and every set of motivations.

As leaders, parents, partners, and even just forward thinkers, there are a million scenarios that we haven't experienced (and never will) that others have been through. Embrace the opportunity to interact with those who have lived differently and see it as a chance to learn from their experiences, both good and bad. It doesn't mean you have to agree with the how they reacted or the viewpoint they gained from the experience. All it means, is that *for the moment*, you grant them the honor of listening to them and putting yourself in their shoes to learn from and better understand them.

This is an area I have had to work very intentionally towards. It meant I had to take personal charge of my open mindedness and become more free and available to everyone I met—not a small undertaking. Even though I don't agree with the ideas or beliefs of many people I meet, I am consciously trying to become more considerate *of their choices.*

This is what has worked for me –

» Giving up control
» Allowing myself to experience new things
» Seeking out all new possibilities
» Empathizing with others
» Learning from my mistakes and the mistakes of others

Giving Up Control –

This can be tough for all of us, but even more so for those of us known as 'Type A' personalities, like myself. We all want to be in control of our lives which is what makes this concept *so much easier* said than done. When we are in control, we feel powerful and safe. We live our lives knowing what to expect from one day to the next. We like that things are being done the way we like them. Who doesn't want that?

Save yourself a lot of time and frustration and anxiety an accept that it is impossible to control every single aspect of your life. It's a blissful concept, but totally unrealistic. Perpetually trying to reach some idealistic level of complete control can even have destructive consequences if we take things too far. It can even take over our lives if we allow it to.

A Personal Turn-out

I have had the opportunity to work for many different types of people over the years and like to think I've been open minded enough to learn a little something from each of them along the way. However, my skills were tested beyond reason by one woman who had to be the most complete control freak I've ever met.

In working with her, I felt like she looked over my shoulder at every juncture, even trying to undermine my every move *just for the sake of control.* She thought it necessary to oversee every single communication before it was delivered to our clients and would waste hours and hours of company time and energy making the most irrelevant changes to a memo I had drafted. When I think back to how her behavior affected me, all it brings back are feelings of anger and frustration. I never felt like she was making valuable contributions or teaching me anything through her changes to my work but that she was just making insignificant changes for the sake of change. She used her position to flex her power in order to leave her 'fingerprints' on everything. Consequently, I lost respect for her and gave up trying so hard to please her. I figured if she was going to find fault regardless of how hard I worked, I'd let her.

My most valuable take-away from working for this woman has helped me in countless situations since then and it's such a simple concept: there are numerous ways to accomplish a task. For almost every single thing we do throughout our lives, there is no single, absolute correct way to accomplish it. Whether it's a major undertaking, like raising a child, or something minor, such as writing a memo, there are an infinite number of ways to go about doing it. So, instead of judging and assuming your way is the right way, *the only way,* let me encourage you to open your mind to different ways of navigating your life.

Believe me, I get it—letting go and giving up control is hard, especially if you are used to taking charge and calling the shots. I am best able to do this when I focus on the bigger, more substantial stuff. I've learned that, if the point I'm trying to make or the way I would do something isn't going to change the outcome of the situation, I don't need to share it. If the memo that you are reviewing looks good and says the right things but is positioned a bit differently than you would write it, leave it as is. Keep in mind the 'don't sweat the small stuff' practice when leading your team members and instead focus on ways that you can add value to them. In doing so, you empower them to think on their own and share their ideas. Your job as a leader is to make your people better and let them grow.

I began this practice with my three kids and it was liberating for all of us. Growing up, their rooms were not always kept spic and span clean. I found myself fighting with them to clean their rooms. I just couldn't understand why they would have some many clothes scattered all over their floor. It bothered me every time I walked by. But one day, I just gave up trying to control how they kept their rooms. I simply closed the door. I still had a nice clean house and I didn't see what was behind those closed doors. The arguing stopped and we were all happier.

Since we're not always going to be able to convince people to change their behavior (at least without some serious resistance!), it is important to put your energies where they are most effective. Don't fight a battle, even if you can win it, if it doesn't have the rewards to justify it. You might ultimately get your way, but the cost can easily overshadow the benefit. Think it through before you gear up for battle. When you give up the minor things of life, you are able to free your mind to focus on the really important matters.

That's not to say that there aren't certain circumstances where it is necessary to take control. It is always your job as a leader to keep in mind the importance of concentrating on the things most critical. The key to this is to understand the difference between the insignificant and the important—a distinction only you can make. Don't allow yourself to be caught up in the power that control can provide.

I've been there, done that, and my closed-minded stance led to arguments that didn't ever need to occur. Fortunately, as I became more enlightened about my life, I was better able to see and understand how my behavior was affecting others. I realized I was maintaining control for the sole purpose of being in control and that it was seriously hindering my ability to be effective. I was losing the respect of those I was trying to lead because I insisted things be done *my way*. Once I made the decision to intentionally make a habit of relinquishing control on things that weren't critical, I became excited to learn the practices and steps that would help me see the difference between the insignificant and the important. It was a complete game-changer in my leadership style. With a more open mind, not only did my two-way communication with others improve dramatically, but so did my two-way growth and learning. I came to appreciate that a confident leader will encourage the growth of others and be open to their ways for accomplishing goals.

Experience New Things –

I can't help it--the desire to experience new things is in my DNA and a driving force in my life. I enjoy putting myself in new situations where I can learn and grow, even if I am stepping into uncontrolled and unknown circumstances. However, I recognize that is not the case for many people and the unknown, coupled with uncertainty, is a scary landscape to live in.

I believe most people are afraid of change and try to avoid situations that can cause discomfort in their everyday lives. I'm not talking about actual physical or mental pain; I'm referring to the discomfort that comes with fear of the unknown. The less adventurous you tend to be, the more likely you are to look at the risk-takers you see and know and tell yourself, "That works for them, but not me. I could never do *that.*"

My personal philosophy is that it is necessary to put yourself in uncomfortable situations for the sole purpose of expanding your mind and staying mentally on your toes. If you make a conscious effort to live outside of your comfort zone, you will be amazed at what you can accomplish. You will be able to achieve things far greater than you ever thought possible.

Not surprisingly, I'm not only comfortable with the uncomfortable, but I'm also a very strong-willed and strong-minded person. I live by the motto, "You are who you think you are." If you believe you will succeed, you've already mentally committed to and accepted the challenge at hand and are willing to do anything in your power to make it happen. Conversely, if you assume you will fail from the beginning and don't give yourself enough confidence and self-respect to accept a challenge, you most assuredly will fail. I am living proof that, if you can teach yourself to have an open mind and an adventurous spirit, you will be richly rewarded with the opportunity to enjoy new experiences and to see the world from a different perspective. I have lived my life looking for those new experiences.

My many examples throughout the book—joining the boy's gymnastics team, becoming a college diver with virtually no previous experience, moving my family half-way across the world to take on a corporate challenge, to finally applying for and being accepted by the greatest reality show of all time, "Survivor"–are all examples of a personal mindset shift to be open to and consider all of life's opportunities.

I look for new experiences. I seek out challenges that allow me to learn and try new things every day. My life would be vastly different today and I would have missed out on so many fabulous things if I had just stayed on the path of certainty and predictability and comfort. My experiences have made me who I am today and have inspired me to help others release their fear of failure, to push themselves to try new adventures, and to commit to constant growth and learning.

And it can all happen when you believe, commit, and achieve!

"If we stay in our comfort zone, we limit our growth; new experiences change our lives."

–Carolyn J. Rivera

Seek out all New Possibilities –

Imagine yourself driving on the open road—a road never ends. There are twists and turns all around you, but for you, there's nothing but the wind in your hair and the sun on your face. And then you realize you must make a decision—you can choose to stay the course on the road you're driving *or take any side road you want.* The choice is completely yours. This is what I happily refer to as having a 'what if…' mentality.

It's really a sort of game except that, instead of traveling on an actual road, you're traveling through *your life.* If you're like me, the endless opportunities are exhilarating. I love nothing more than to consider the 'what ifs' of my life because I see my days on earth as an open road before me—with no limit or end in sight.

Ask yourself how *your life* would be different if you adopted this 'what if' frame of mind. Imagine all the wonderful things that could be just around the next turn if you allow yourself to believe in what is possible. Or if you allowed yourself to see past the obvious right in front of you and intentionally made different choices.

I'm not, by any means, challenging you to be cavalier about your life or to change just for the sake of changing. You should always have a compelling reason to change. However, that doesn't mean that you shouldn't, at least occasionally, trade in all the surroundings on the road—*your road*—for an unexpected and out of the ordinary twist or turn that piques your interest.

Be cautious not to use the 'what if' considerations to feed your insecurities or take you to a worst-case scenario. It can be far too easy to focus our minds on all the things that can prevent us from succeeding instead of the opportunities waiting to be discovered. This kind of thinking is destructive and will surely hinder your ability to free your mind and grow in a positive direction. Along the same lines, don't fall into the trap of allowing those around you to do likewise. Those who are first to shoot down your dreams and ideas are the very ones who are perpetually content with the status quo and who have little desire to grow beyond *their personal comfort zone.*

Your full potential in life cannot be achieved while living life in your comfort zone. I challenge you to break out of yours and free your mind to see the possibilities in your life. You owe it to yourself to maintain positivity in your life and surround yourself with people who aren't consumed with failure. You become the people who you are around the most. If you are with people with open minds and who are looking to improve and to see the possibilities *in their own lives*, you will want to do the same. If you are hanging around with those that are comfortable with the monotony of day to day existence, then that likely is *where you will stay.* The choice is yours. I challenge you to take action to look for mentors who share your vision and outlook on life. Be curious. And never stop searching for new and different and challenging ways to grow.

Empathize with Others –

Empathy is the ability to imagine yourself in another person's situation and feel their emotions as if you were in their situation. On the surface, it seems like empathy should be second nature to us as humans. We all feel pain, and even though we may not be feeling pain at a particular moment, we remember the realness of it. Shouldn't it follow that we can easily empathize with someone who is feeling pain at the moment? Usually not. Despite so many of our shared emotions and feelings, feeling true empathy for others can be difficult for some people.

When we understand the importance of empathy in building and maintaining relationships, we intentionally try to put ourselves in other's shoes and be of comfort to them. Unfortunately, there are times when we just can't fully relate. We can empathize with the feeling of pain, but not necessarily *their* type of pain or to *their* extent, because we simply haven't felt what they are feeling.

We all process and react to painful situations differently. For some of us, our natural reaction to pain is sadness. For others, it might be anger or a feeling of self-doubt. Unless we have been through something similar to what someone else is feeling, having true empathy can be hard. I've had lots of experiences when I *wanted* to be fully empathetic with a friend or loved one, but because I hadn't experienced anything like what they are going through, I felt like my efforts fell short.

I have a person in my life that has been chronically unhappy as long as I've known him. It doesn't matter the decade or the year or the month because he is always under a cloud of depression, self-loathing, and self-pity. It's not that he's always in a bad mood or sad or grouchy, because on the surface, he isn't. But if you take the time to get into a personal conversation with him, his real emotions become evident very quickly.

A few years ago we were having one of those 'woe is me' conversations and I was empathizing in the ways I always had with him—*the only way I knew to do so*. Naturally, I've always wanted him to find happiness in his life, but this time I could see that his feelings were clearly hurt by my attempts to empathize and offer advice for change. Seeing the hurt in his eyes made me feel horrible. From that moment forward, I realized that I needed to improve my approach to being empathetic. I quit offering advice and just listened, offering emotional support instead of practical advice. That was the moment I learned that empathy doesn't necessarily mean you need to offer a solution or try to fix the problem; it mostly means you validate the person and their feelings. Since then, our conversations have become significantly more fulfilling *for both of us*.

I've had many conversations with him through the years, and all he can see is the doom and gloom of life. He is unhappy in his job, can't seem to find the right relationship, feels like his life is going nowhere, and feels like he hasn't accomplished anything meaningful. But because I can't understand the depth of his problems, I see his life differently. I see that he has been successful but has maybe given up. I see that he has accomplished very meaningful things but has chosen not to continue to do so recently. I have tried repeatedly to put myself in his shoes and empathize with his situation, but to be completely honest, my mind just doesn't work like his. I can't even imagine having such a tragic outlook on life because I have *intentionally* chosen to live a happy and fulfilling life. I have also learned to handle the negative feelings that occasionally surface in my own life to spur me on to make conscious changes. I've had to make peace with my friend's pessimistic mind set and to do what I can—offer an attentive ear, a hug, and my friendship and be as empathetic as I can.

Empathy is important, but genuine empathy is required if you want to build and maintain relationships. If you have gone through a similar experience, your empathy will be genuine. If you haven't, it's okay to say that you haven't experienced their pain but can understand how painful it must be for them. If you find yourself at a loss as to how to best empathize with someone, do the next best thing—offer your genuine friendship and love. Every situation is unique when it comes to being empathetic, but it is invaluable for building strong relationships with family, friends, and those you lead.

Learn From Your Mistakes –

The greatest lessons learned in life are those that result from our failures. We've all experienced failure at something and recall the awful feeling. This alone should be enough incentive to learn from our mistakes, but the real learning comes when we take the time to examine the missteps if we want to ensure we don't repeat them.

A Personal Turn-out

There was a time in my life when I was not ready to learn or open to instruction. This ultimately meant I had to learn everything the hard way. I had a great job at a company I truly enjoyed working for and life was good in the moment. I was working my way up quickly in the organization, I enjoyed my supervisor, and the work was fulfilling. All was well in my world.

One day my reporting structure changed and I was assigned a new supervisor—one that had a reputation within the company for being impossible to deal with. No problem, I thought. I had built a great reputation within the company and figured I could get my supervisor assignment changed with little effort. I was wrong—very wrong.

Foolishly, instead of trying to be open minded and forming my own opinion of him, I took a different approach. I just ignored him and his authority and went about my business. I only checked in with him when I was required to, effectively sabotaging *my own position* at a company I really liked. I was so close-minded, I didn't even try to make it work. I actually thought I was invincible.

When I look back on that experience, I realize I clearly should have done *so many things* differently. If had been capable of putting my ego aside and given my supervisor a chance, things would have worked out so much differently. I had basically given up before I ever got started with him. I bypassed the need to establish a relationship with him and went directly to judging him. My behavior cost me a fulfilling job where I truly was making a difference. My over-active ego and unwillingness to be open minded was my undoing.

Later, when I realized how poorly I had handled the situation, I was embarrassed and upset. I blew that opportunity all on my own and I'm not proud of it. The upside is that I learned a great lesson from my mistake.

I truly believe we learn and grow more from our failures than our successes. We all are faced with challenges throughout life. The difference in the outcomes is based largely upon how we approach them. If we see each situation with an open mind and give it a chance for success, the opportunity to overcome the difficulty will always remain. There's hope in our failures…and opportunity.

The old adage, 'fool me once, shame on you; fool me twice, shame on me,' is never more applicable than in handling our mistakes. I take this wisdom very seriously to heart. I have since learned that, if I don't put in the effort to analyze and learn from my mistakes and find myself in the same failed situation again, there is no one to blame but myself. I know it can be painful to re-hash our failures, but these are the questions I ask myself whenever I am faced with failures –

» What was the goal or expected outcome?
» Was the goal clearly defined and realistic or more idealistic?
» Did I follow the plan that I put in place to achieve the goal?
» Was the timing of the goal the right?
» Did I face obstacles that I could have prevented?

- » Was I flexible?
- » Did my ego affect the outcome?
- » Did I commit 100%?
- » Were there external factors beyond my control that I didn't account for which prevented me from achieving my goal?
- » Ultimately, why did I fail?
- » What can I learn from my failure?
- » How will I prevent this failure from happening again?

It is a lot of questions, I know, but each of them relates directly back to defining your vision and each step in the process to ultimate success. By asking yourself these questions, you will be able to convert your failures into learning experiences, effectively changing what was first considered a loss into a win! And the bonus is that you won't be near as likely to make those same mistakes again.

Now you're in the best possible position to take your new-found knowledge and apply it to the next goal. Don't dwell on what has been. Learn from it, work to become more open minded, and move on to what can be!

Reflection –

How far are you willing to go to achieve open-mindedness? I urge you to dig deep, to start small and grow big, to surround yourself with those that support you, to seek out opportunities for growth with eyes wide open, and to take each failure with a sense of pride because you are a better person having learned from it.

"In my first season of 'Survivor,' Season 29, 'Blood vs. Water II,' I was set in my ways and not very flexible working with any and every one of my castmates. I formed my alliance and thought I would be able to ride through the game and solely work with that one alliance. This strategy got me a 10th place finish, a trip to Ponderosa, and a cozy seat on the jury.

Going into Season 31, 'Second Chances Cambodia,' I wanted to play more of a carefree and erratic game. I wanted to set aside emotions and be open minded to work with everyone. This strategy worked perfectly with S31 because that was the birth of voting blocs.

Voting blocs are when groups of people form alliances for one vote on one night. Being open minded gave me the liberty to move from voting bloc to voting bloc and not only vote former allies out, but also being open to playing with castmates who had blindsided me and voted out people in my temporary alliance.

Without being open minded, I would never have worked with those that lied to me and would never have voted off those who were, at one point, working with me…and thus, never had won the title of 'Sole Survivor.'

–Jeremy Collins
"Survivor" Winner, Season 31
Koh Rong, Cambodia, 'Second Chances'

Bamboo is super strong. To win in 'Survivor,'
you have to build strong relationships,
just as you do throughout life.

R is for Relationships

Relationship-building is the foundation of society as we know it. In the times of early man, even before humans had a common form of communication, they recognized the need for each other just in order to survive and to live a better life. As a result, they formed clans for protection, learned to hunt together for a greater chance of success, divided up tasks for greater efficiency, and shared ideas on tools, food, and clothing. None of these things would have been possible had they not built relationships among one another. Despite their primitive ways, people understood 'it takes a village' if you hope to do more than just survive. Relationships make *everything* happen.

Fast forward a few thousand years, and while our lifestyles have changed drastically, our need for relationships is still very much present. Considering that our ancestors were able to form relationships without even a common language between them, I have to believe that the need for relationships is in our DNA. We are born knowing how to build them.

That said, we should recognize there are many different types of relationships, all with varying degrees of depth and longevity. We have personal relationships with our family and loved ones that we nurture constantly and that typically span a lifetime. We also have professional relationships which may be present for a season or longer and that affect our career trajectory.

Relationship building is a critical skill that directly correlates to success in life, both personally and professionally. As we established earlier in the book, alone, none of us have the power, experience, or bandwidth to accomplish our vision. All of us must build a network of inspired champions to accomplish our goals at work and at home. Your inspired champions should be the people in your life you are most comfortable collaborating and communicating with; they should also be open-minded and open to the inspiration your vision should provide.

I believe relationship building is both an art and a science. It is an art because our communication skills need to be intriguing, graceful, patient, and attentive. It is a science because it requires a specific approach to effectively communicate the parameters, needs, and expectations of the relationship.

Relationships require some basis of connection between people—a shared vision, a common belief, or a mutual likeness of something. That's a solid beginning, but to create a lasting and mutually beneficial relationship with others, it takes concerted initiative and the passage of time. Relationships don't just happen.

Sure, some spring up initially due to circumstances or chance, but at a certain point for a relationship to continue, you must recognize a mutual purpose or need to be filled. When this happens, your relationship takes on structure and is no longer 'just happening.' Otherwise, there would be no need for the relationship to continue.

Relationship-building, at its core, is focused on understanding, learning, and becoming familiar with another person. If you use your art of communication to take the time to listen and understand what drives a person, you can then apply the science of communication toward a vision or other mutual benefits. Often, we try to build a relationship without respecting all that we must do in order to establish a solid foundation. We rush through, or even try to avoid, the 'getting to know you' part (the art) and instead put our focus on the 'here's what I want from this relationship' (the science) part.

To build a strong relationship, you must forget about yourself for a little bit. Allow yourself to be taken in, interested, and open-minded about what the other person is telling you. You might even learn something through this process! Think about a past conversation—one in which you knew the other person wasn't listening *at all*. Do you think they weren't listening because you were boring? Probably not. Chances are, they weren't listening because they were more interested in their own agenda and just waiting their turn to speak. It is nearly impossible to build a connection with someone who is only concerned with what they bring to or want from the relationship.

Building long-lasting relationships must have a foundation of trust, understanding, empathy, and genuine connection. Add to that the fact that relationships are usually very complex and subject to frequent and quickly-changing dynamics. To get you started on the right path towards developing long and meaningful relationships here are a few suggestions –

Be Genuine –

What seems obvious to most of us can still be a hurdle some people just can't clear. Most of us can see right through someone not being genuine when their motives come to light. Fakers can only keep the act up so long without revealing their true selves. Real relationships are deep and committed and cannot be based upon superficial and false personas. That's why it's important to get to know someone before you invest the time and effort that strong relationships must have to flourish.

Ask yourself these questions before you determine if a potential relationship is worth your investment –

 » What do we have in common?
 » Do we value the same things?
 » What is the best method for us to connect and what can we bond over?
 » What is it about this person that intrigues me and makes me want to get to know them better?

After you consider these questions you will have a better understanding of the potential for the relationship and can move forward from there.

Build Trust –

It bears repeating that building relationships are rooted in trust. Building trust takes time and is based more on actions than words. People need to know how much you care about them and that they can rely upon you in good times and bad. When you think about the strongest relationships in your life, think about what you have done to strengthen the trust between you and the other person. Have you been supportive of them? Are they confident you will continue to be available for them if needed? Trust grows when your support is consistent.

Focus on Their Needs –

We usually enter into relationships because of a need or desire *on our part*. We might even target who we want to form a relationship with. At face value that may even seem a little calculating, but it is a relationship fact of life. To be clear, you must be your genuine self in your pursuit of a relationship with someone, but it doesn't mean you can't be a little intentional when deciding who and for what reason you want to initiate a relationship.

Whether we admit it or not, we all have relational needs. True relationship builders are committed to focusing on the needs of others and not waiting on others to do the same for them. Whether your relationship is in a professional environment or personal, people need to know you are tuned in to their needs and genuinely care. None of us are owed anything in a relationship and the only way to succeed in building a lasting one is to focus on the other person. No doubt you've heard John Maxwell's famous quote, "people don't care how much you know until they know how much you care." It has stood the test of time because it's true. To master the relationships in your life, focus on the needs of others, first, and your success second.

Think about how this might apply towards making a major purchase such as a car. Most of the time, you can just tell when a salesperson is really working you over—either sooner or later as you talk with them. It's a total turn-off and a conversation you wouldn't even be engaging in except that they stand in the way between you and a new set of wheels.

As soon as you entered the dealership, did they initiate a real conversation with you or did it feel like you were being pounced upon? Did you feel like they were interested in your needs or just making a sale and reaching their quota? In my experience, most salespeople usually initiate the conversation by stating what *they* have to offer and what *they* have on sale. But, if they took a moment to ask what I'm interested in buying and what my needs were, it would be so much more effective. When they focus on *their* agenda and try to sell what *they* want to sell, the responsibility for sharing my needs and preferences falls *on me*. When salespeople allow their focus on making a sale to overshadow the investment of time into finding out what their customer needs and wants, it can be counterproductive— either missing the sale completely or, at least, sacrificing the possibility of future sales *with the same customer*.

The potential opportunity cost lost from not building a relationship can be a blind spot for lots of us—especially with a career based on sales. I understand the importance of meeting sales quotas, but I also know they shouldn't come at the expense of investing in customers.

If you remain empathetic and open-minded with others and work to engage them in two-way communication, your track record for success will last much longer than those who focus primarily upon themselves. They might make a quicker sale, but you'll enjoy the long-term payoff of a relationship and probably repeat interest and business and referrals. Whether you're selling cars, gadgets, or an idea to a conference room full of executives, when others are confident that you have their best interests at heart, they will give more serious thought to 'buying what you're selling.'

Building better relationships can usually be accomplished by following a simple, but thoughtful, process. Before you start talking about yourself and your needs in any relationship, make it a point to find out four specific things about the person you are talking to. Listen closely to what they say and then work to build a connection with them based upon the details you have uncovered. This requires you to listen very intentionally to what they say and how they say it.

Let them know that you are interested in their success, whether it's on a professional level or personally. When you do this, your respect, accountability, and influence are all raised significantly with this person because you're committing to help them, not just now, but also in the future. If you are available and truly care for people when they have a need, it will have a lasting impact on both of your lives and will strengthen the relationship tremendously. It's such a simple concept, but one so few people give much attention to—focus on others, be selfless, and always remember the relationship is not all about you!

It becomes much easier to invest in and commit to others when you make these practices a part of your relationship-building skills.

Stop Keeping Score –

Most of us do nice things for people we have built relationships with, sometimes without them even asking. These are considered favors because they require something of us and they benefit someone else. Favors can be a natural validation of a strong relationship. It is a give-and-take system of service that works best when it's kept in balance. However, sometimes these favors can get a little bit lopsided, leaving one party feeling taken advantage of. If we're the ones doing the favors time after time and begin to feel slighted, it's usually because we are giving or doing with the expectation that our actions will be reciprocated. Even when we don't necessarily keep track one-for-one, we can still eventually come to expect something in return.

When we do this, subconsciously or consciously, it can become unhealthy and eventually damage the relationship. Life isn't a one-for-one sport. Don't do something for another person with the expectation of having it repaid. If you only give to get, you could save yourself some time and just give yourself what you want in the first place.

However, be careful not to confuse favors with transactions. There are situations where it is very clear that you have something another person wants or needs done and maybe you agree to 'divide and conquer' based on a certain set of parameters. For example, you offer to do the laundry if I'll wash the dishes. In these kind of transactions, the expectations and the roles are clear. Just remember, relationships are not transactions and deserve not to be treated as such.

If you are comfortable in a relationship and want to give freely, do so. But if you start to tally up what you've done for the other person versus what they have done for you, it's probably time to rethink your intentions for doing favors. Left unchecked, this internal scorecard can lead to resentment—*all based upon something that should have been given without expectations.* If you want or need something from someone else, it is so much better to ask outright rather than stew and become angry when your needs are not met.

Ironically, most of the time when we do things for others, *they want to reciprocate.* When someone performs a selfless act on my behalf or for my benefit, I am usually overwhelmed with happiness and inspired to do something kind in return. It may not be one-for-one or immediate, but I truly want to return the kindness.

Respect the Opinions of Others –

Giving respect to the opinions of others can be quite a challenge—especially when they don't align with ours. By the time we are adults most of us have formed some fairly concrete opinions about the things that make us who we are. They are based on our life experiences, how we were educated, and our natural personality tendencies.

Some of our opinions are deep seated and not easily changed. That's not my point at all. Under no circumstances are you obligated to believe or accept the opinions of others. You should, however, allow them the courtesy of listening to them and respecting them. This is where you have the opportunity to practice keeping an open mind.

In terms of relationships, we've discussed that it is just natural to have better connections with those who have similar beliefs and opinions. But don't allow this inclination to discourage you from having relationships with those you don't see exactly eye-to-eye with. Relationships of this nature are great learning opportunities. They give us insights and ideas and perspectives we might never have considered otherwise.

To better understand how to show respect towards people's opinions we don't readily share, it's usually helpful to figure out why we feel the way we do. What formed our opinion in the first place? What stands in the way of us respecting their point of view?

Because I'm such a logical person and much of my personality is rooted in fact and understanding, I immediately become frustrated when I talk with someone with a very solid opinion on a topic 'just because.' I have a hard time respecting this way of thinking. I have always believed, if you have an opinion, you should be able to explain why you feel that way and how you educated yourself on the topic to arrive at your opinion.

It is also difficult for me to respect an opinion when it appears to me as racist, sexist, or rooted in fear or anger. Even though it's a struggle for me to understand such a viewpoint, I work to keep an open mind whenever I meet people with such opinions. It doesn't mean that I ever come to agree with them, but I can practice being respectful of their right to feel as they do. I also have to occasionally remind myself that I don't have to build a relationship with everyone I meet, but I should always work to be respectful of them.

Open and Honest Communication –

To be genuine, you must be honest in your communications. There are very few situations where telling someone what they want to hear, rather than the truth, is helpful. Even though some things may be difficult to say, don't use it as an excuse to withhold information or tell the complete story. If you do, you run the risk of the person eventually learning the complete truth and feeling betrayed or disrespected because you wanted to spare their feelings and were afraid to be honest with them. This can be one of the hardest things you'll ever do. No doubt, it takes courage in these situations, but it is the right thing to do.

A Personal Turn-out

I can recall a situation where I had been hearing some information shared about of friend of mine at work. It was a very touchy subject—personal hygiene. The talk was that this individual had serious body odor. It reached the point where I felt like I had to have a conversation with this person about it.

Imagine my discomfort at having to tell someone not only did they have body odor, but that others were talking about it. It was just as horrible as it sounds. But when I considered how they would feel if they found out I knew about the office talk and still didn't tell them, I knew I had to do something. I also took into consideration that, if the situation were the other way around—if I were the one with the issue—I would absolutely want to know.

I followed through, had the conversation, and the individual cried. I felt terrible. In the end, though, it was something that needed to be done and it made our relationship stronger because it showed I truly cared. It showed that I didn't want people talking about this individual for things that could be controlled. It showed that I didn't want the reputation of that individual to be focused on something so trivial.

Sometimes open and honest communication requires you to get completely out of your comfort zone and focus squarely on others. It's better to encourage people to speak openly and honestly than to learn there was an issue later on—especially if it helps you grow and better yourself.

There's also the possibility that we're completely wrong about something, that our information is outdated or our source unreliable. Whatever the reason for the misinformation, if no one corrects us, we'll simply continue to believe we're right when *we're actually very wrong*. Take the risk of being uncomfortable and share the correction. You would want someone to do so for you.

I've had long conversations with people only to realize hours later that I had toilet paper stuck to my shoe, or my blouse was miss-buttoned, or that I'd called the other person the wrong name for the entire conversation. I would have been so grateful early on if someone—*anyone*—had the courage to pull me aside and let me know. I could have fixed the problem and gone on instead of going through the day with something not quite right and never knowing about it.

Clearly, these scenarios aren't easy to talk about. I've been on both the telling end of the conversation and the receiving end. Most of the time, either side is uncomfortable, *but only for a minute.* I would *always* want to know if I'm the one in the embarrassing situation and I think most other people would, too. Sometimes building and maintaining strong relationships demands this of us, but that is what open and honest communication is all about.

As we've discussed, building relationships demands a lot from us. It requires focus, listening, and two-way communication. Successful relationships are mutual. Both parties understand their role and the intent or desire of the relationship. Both parties stand to benefit from solid relationships, too. If all of these qualities aren't present, it's more likely you have merely an acquaintance and not a strong and rewarding relationship with another person.

Reflection

Look over your contact list and determine which people you have a relationship with and those that are simply acquaintances. Then practice these suggested steps and watch as the acquaintances strengthen and deepen to point of becoming full-fledged and mutually beneficial relationships. Your future, either professional and/or personally, will be richer for the investment of time and energy.

"True relationships take time to build, but once you do, they are long-lasting. The key is to listen and hear what people are saying. Everyone wants to be heard and feel like they matter. I believe that successful leaders are those that truly care about people.

In the game of 'Survivor,' this becomes so important because there are so many people trying to take the lead.

When you show others you care about them, you are building that bond forever."

–Michele Fitzgerald
"Survivor" Winner, Season 32
Kaoh Rong, Cambodia, "Kaoh Rong"

With the immunity necklace around your neck on 'Survivor,' you are safe from the vote and one step closer to winning the game. You always win when you achieve VICTORY!

Yielding Results

Y is for Yielding Results

The culmination of this whole V-I-C-T-O-R-Y process is to yield results. It's the end game, the finish line, the goal you're striving for. For our purposes, results can best be described as the successful completion of your vision, meaning you achieved the expected outcomes based upon the standards you set from the beginning.

As you'll recall from the start of this journey, your expected outcomes and results should be clearly defined and as objective as possible. Don't leave what is important to you open to subjective interpretation. This may sound harsh, but without documented and measurable results, you can easily rationalize approximations, even vague estimates, and not have a clear measure of success.

Too often, many people overlook this critical step. On the surface, it can seem like an unnecessary task. After all, won't you recognize success when you see it? Not necessarily. A lack of definition allows for an undefined end to a vision. This can be dangerous territory because it gives way to procrastinating or dragging out the whole process if you don't know when and where and how you will achieve success. If you don't know where the finish line is, you never know when the race is over.

Without an objective measure of accomplishment, even the most committed among us will eventually give up, assume we're done and consider the whole experience a success *whether it is or not*. Mentally, it is important to have that finality and closure even if there is a Part Two to your vision. When you close the chapter and recognize the success of achieving Part One, you set yourself up to better take on Part Two.

It is up to you to decide how you will measure the success of your vision, but it is helpful to know there are several ways to go about it. For example, if your vision is to write a book, you might consider success several different ways, none of which are wrong. The obvious one would be simply that your book is published, either by a large publishing house or independently. One takes a whole lot more effort and networking than the other, but both result in a published book. If you're more ambitious, maybe success really means you land on the New York Times Best Seller. Or, if your primary purpose for writing the book is to help others and you receive mounds of positive feedback and testimonies about the positive impact your book has upon people, that would also be a worthy measurement of success also. The point is, whatever your personal measure of success, set the parameters from the start so you can recognize the victory and allow it to spur you on to fulfilling your next vision.

A Personal Turn-Out

One of my personal examples of measuring my success in the past has been related to the numerous training programs I was hired to develop for companies. The end goal for me at the end of my training programs was to achieve a behavior change from those who participated. I measured this with a before-and-after standard. If employees performed a task different and/or better after the training, I considered it a success. If they reverted back to their old ways, I had not succeeded in changing their behavior. These results were measurable and verifiable. However, some companies I worked for only wanted to measure success from the standpoint of whether their employees completed the training. Their minds may have been a million miles away, but if they were present during the entire program, they received credit for completion. I personally didn't consider this a valid measure of success because there was no connection made between changed behavior and participation in my class. I always recommended incorporating a way to track behavior before I presented the program and a way to monitor it afterward. This allowed me and the executives who hired me to see the difference the training made and how it directly (and positively) linked back to accomplishing the organizational goals and objectives.

One last example to illustrate this – Assume you were hired to deliver a training program for a company that makes and sells mattresses. They have a new product for sale and need to educate their employees on the product features as well as give them the tools they need to sell the mattresses—essentially linking the product features to benefits that directly impact customers and increase their ultimate satisfaction.

The first measurement of success for your training program would be to ensure that every person who took the training completely understands the new product and is able to tout the benefits to a potential customer. One way to measure an employee's understanding could be through a mandatory quiz over the features and benefits of the product and best practices for how to position it to customers. By requiring all employees pass a competency test on the new product, you have a clear understanding of your employees' understanding of the benefits and the expectations of them in the sales process.

Once you've tested and documented that the employees understand the product features and benefits, the next point of measurement would probably be to determine whether or not the message is well received by the customer. After all, the main objective here is to satisfy the needs of the customers and increase their satisfaction. To do so, you would need a measurement to determine how customers feel about the product and if it satisfies their needs. This would likely be a two-pronged evaluation—first, to determine whether the employee is effectively delivering the product message to the customer or not; and secondly, to determine the satisfaction level of the customers. Both of these evaluations could be handled relatively easily—through monitoring employee presentations and customer surveys, respectively. Armed with observation, testing, customer feedback, and sales, you are now in a position

to truly evaluate the success of the training program to introduce a new product.

Overall, it doesn't have to be difficult to determine the means of measurement for your vision or even the process of taking these measurements; it just requires time and forethought to set programs in place from the beginning. If you don't set the standard for measure, you won't see change, either because your results are too vague or there's a lack of accountability that diminishes the results. If you don't take the time to declare what will be measured, how it will be measured, and why it is being measured, and the importance of these measurements, those participating won't see the process as important either.

"You get what you measure."

–Carolyn J. Rivera

Reflection –

Think through the possibilities for how to measure your results. Will it be through increased sales, changed behaviors, satisfaction level, or something else? Use your results to help you see what parameters need to be met before you can claim success and move on to your next vision.

"In 'Game Changers,' I changed my game. I focused on the things I needed to do differently to win. You can do anything you set your mind to—even the ordinary can achieve the extraordinary!"

–Sarah Lacina
"Survivor" Winner, Season 34
Cagayan, Philippines, "Game Changers"

Vision

Influence

Communiucation

Trust

Open-mindedness

Relationships

Yield Results

Summary

Everyone of us has the skills, perspecitve, experiences and ideas that can be used to help others. Leadership is providing value to others.

Leadership is a dynamic practice that requires us to constantly look for ways to improve, learn and grow.

This book is dedicated to helping you achieve VICTORY. Now the ball is in your court. I challenge you to take it and run with it and share with me your countless VICTORIES!

Believe Commit Achieve

End Notes

1. Training Magazine, 2013, https://trainingmag.com/four-types-leaders, Accessed 14 September 2016.

2. Harvard Business Review, 1996, https://hbr.org/1996/09/building-your-companys-vision, Accessed 24 October 2016.

For more information about Carolyn or if you would like to have her speak at your organization please visit: **CarolynJRivera.com**.

PLANT Your FLAG

THE SEVEN SECRETS TO WINNING

CPSIA information can be obtained
at www.ICGtesting.com
Printed in the USA
BVHW031143240220
573151BV00001B/32